The Design and Production of Self-Instructional Materials

Open and Distance Learning Series

Series Editor: Fred Lockwood

OPEN AND DISTANCE LEARNING SERIES

The Design and Production of Self-Instructional Materials

FRED LOCKWOOD

KOGAN PAGE

YOURS TO HAVE AND TO HOLD

BUT NOT TO COPY

First published in 1998

Apart from any fair dealing for the purposes of research or private study, or criticism or review, as permitted under the Copyright, Designs and Patents Act 1988, this publication may only be reproduced, stored or transmitted, in any form or by any means, with the prior permission in writing of the publishers, or in the case of reprographic reproduction in accordance with the terms and licences issued by the CLA. Enquiries concerning reproduction outside these terms should be sent to the publishers at the undermentioned address.

Kogan Page Limited
120 Pentonville Road
London
N1 9JN
UK

Stylus Publishing Inc.
22883 Quicksilver Drive
Sterling
VA 20166-2012
USA

British Library Cataloguing in Publication Data

A CIP record for this book is available from the British Library.

ISBN 0 7494 1455 3

Typeset by Kogan Page
Printed and bound in Great Britain by Biddles Ltd, Guildford and King's Lynn

Contents

Preface

Within the UK it is likely that in every school or college, factory or office, hospital or agency there is someone working there, or a relative or friend, who is following a self-instructional course or some form of training involving self-instructional materials. The growth in the use of such materials in teaching and training over the last 25 years has been phenomenal. The impact of the Open College and Open University in the UK has been immense. Indeed, future books in the Open and Distance Learning Series will focus on *Open and Distance Learning in Schools* and *Open and Flexible Learning in Vocational Education and Training*. Organizations as diverse as Rover Cars and National Westminster Bank, the Police Force and British Gas, the Inland Revenue and the Society of Cosmetic Scientists train and retrain their staff using self-instructional materials. The growth in the use of self-instructional materials around the world in recent years has also gathered pace. Open schools have been developed in India and Indonesia and are planned for elsewhere. New Open Universities have been established in South America, the Far East, Southern Africa and Europe. The training and retraining of staff in industry, commerce and the social services are increasing rapidly. But who trains the trainers?

In 1985 the Open University (OU) published the package *Making Self-Instructional Material for Adults*. The multimedia package incorporated two five-day workshops, weeks or months apart, conducted by an OU staff member and designed to help participants plan, produce and present their own self-instructional materials. I conducted these training sessions, but unfortunately the course had a short life and was withdrawn years ago. However, I continued to conduct face-to-face workshops, and to develop seminars, games and simulations with groups across a broad spectrum of academic and technical areas – both in the UK and overseas. Indeed, in the last five years alone I have conducted training courses in the design of self-instructional materials in 15 countries and at over 80 venues; these have ranged from one-day to two-week programmes. During these training sessions I became increasingly aware that only so many sessions could be conducted in the time available – and often not all who wanted to attend could do so. The logical solution was to transform the face-to-face activities into a self-instructional form so that individuals could work through them on their own or so that one or more people could use them to create their own training materials.

This book, *The Design and Production of Self-Instructional Materials* is based on training sessions I have conducted on dozens of occasions with hundreds of participants – I believe they are foolproof and virtually 'run themselves'. They focus on those areas that I believe are key to the design of self-instructional materials – an awareness of the distinctive features of self-instructional materials, the characteristics of your target audience and coming to grips with the resources and constraints within which you must work. The materials offered will enable you to consider alternative ways of producing your teaching material and to provide a framework within which you can assemble a course proposal. Other chapters will provide key questions and resources that will allow you to assemble advance organizers, estimate student workload and devise learning activities. I suspect you will want to replace some of the questions I offer, add your own examples and convert some workshops into seminars and others into games or simulations. However you use this resource, I hope that you, your colleagues and learners benefit.

It is likely that I will continue to conduct training sessions based on these materials – to refine them and develop others. I would welcome your comments and suggestions as to how they can be improved.

Fred Lockwood

Ways of using the guidelines – for individual or group use

You have a decision to make. Are you going to treat this book as self-instructional material or as a series of ready-made workshops? Do you really have any choice? Not everyone is fortunate enough to have colleagues who are interested or involved in producing material to be studied in an open, distance or flexible learning context. I'm aware that many teachers and trainers are working on their own with little support and encouragement. If you are in this position you may have no choice but to treat the book as a form of self-instructional material. If so, I would suggest that you skim the next paragraph and go the section entitled 'Self-instructional material'.

Of course you may be part of group or department that is involved, or is going to be involved, in producing such material, and you thus have a great opportunity to share your experiences and stimulate each other. If you are thinking about getting a small group together I would suggest you read through the series of practical points I raise in the section entitled 'Ready made workshops'.

Self-instructional material

If you are going to regard the various chapters as a form of self-instructional material the following comments may help you. The opening paragraph(s) of each chapter will provide an overview of the chapter; it will orientate you to the major issue that I feel you will need to address and resolve. The subsequent key questions are those that have arisen in literally dozens of workshops and seminars and which I feel are the most important ones to address and resolve. If you were to spend two minutes *brainstorming* these questions it would be a valuable way of generating your own ideas and starting to think of the implications they have for you in your situation. You could then compare your ideas with the comments I have assembled and decide on the extent to which they agree, disagree or require further consideration. For many of the comments associated with the key questions I have assembled quotes, extracts, examples and illustrations. In every case I have summarized the points on a single page as a potential overhead projector transparency. At the end of each chapter I have listed two or three sources of information.

I would estimate that you could read through the opening statement, brainstorm the key questions, compare my comments with yours and decide your future course of action in 20–30 minutes per chapter. It really could be time well spent.

Ready-made workshops

Each of the following workshops has been developed and refined over a number of years, to a point where I think they are virtually foolproof. In fact, in recent years I have invited colleagues to take a particular workshop booklet, read through it, and conduct the workshop on my behalf. On many occasions they have simply posed the questions I have offered, drawn upon the discussion points listed and adopted the time allocations I have indicated. At other times they have rephrased one or more of the questions, added discussion points and varied the time allocations – as I am sure you will want to do. On some occasions the participants provided unexpected suggestions which enhanced the original workshop's plan. I have incorporated these into the workshops that are presented, but you may find occasional points raised that were not expected and which give that added zest to the event. However, in every case the workshops presented – questions, discussion points and time allocations – have proved to be extremely robust.

Number of participants

I have conducted the following workshops with as few as four and as many as 80 participants; for both extremes it is fairly hard work! Of course, you may have no control over the number of participants taking part, but if you do I would suggest between 20 and 30. This is enough to form four or five small groups and to give you some flexibility in which groups report back – as well as ensuring you are likely to have a sufficient number to generate the sort of responses you need to address each of the questions posed. Twenty to 30 people also generate a certain productive 'hum' when they are chatting together to meet the tight deadline you will have given them.

Workshop venue

I have had the misfortune, on several occasions, to be allocated a lecture theatre in which to conduct a workshop – complete with fixed, tiered seating! With groups sat in the aisles, on the top of 'foldaway' worktops and with twisted necks I've managed – but it is not recommended. Any room large enough to accommodate participants sitting comfortably is usually acceptable. I used to think that the ideal was a large room for everyone, but with a series of smaller, syndicate rooms within easy reach to which small groups could move and discuss particular questions. However, there is a real danger that, in having so much movement during the workshop, it becomes like musical chairs, detracting from the main purpose of the workshop and consuming valuable time. The saving in time more than compensates for the increased level of noise – provided the acoustics are not awful!

Allocation to small groups

You may have your own way of forming small groups of participants for your workshops. If you are happy with it then continue to use it. However, you may find it interesting to try one or more different ways.

Assuming you have an adequately sized room, the laziest way is simply to group the people into those clusters where they are sitting, be they groups of four or five, six or seven. It is certainly quick and may capitalize on the phenomena that those colleagues who feel comfortable in each other's company tend to sit together automatically. Alternatively, you could plan the room beforehand, removing spare tables and chairs so as to make more use of the space that you do have available. However, if you think that positioning six chairs around each table will result in neat small groups of six people you are going to be disappointed. Many will, though, fall into this arrangement, and a little cajoling will normally result in the group size and positions you want.

You may wish to ensure that the groups are randomly allocated, evenly balanced in terms of the proportions of men and women in each group. The most efficient way I have found is to check the number of men and women in the whole group and by simple arithmetic work out how many groups you can form with, say, six people per group. For example, if there were 12 women and 18 men (total of 30 participants) you could form five groups of six people. When announcing to the participants that you want to group them so that there is an even distribution of men and women in each group I have never had any dissent. It is then easy to say you are going to allocate them to one of five groups by number – with each group being represented by a number.

Starting with the women give each one a number from 1 to 5. I have found that this works best by asking the women, in turn, to call out their group number (and to remember it!) as you make eye contact with them as you move around the room systematically. This would result in groups 1, 2 and 3 having three women in them and groups 4 and 5 only two. All you need to do next is to repeat the sequence with the male participants, but starting the allocation with group number 4. This will ensure that you have mixed sex groups with the best balance you can achieve. You can then designate a particular table or area of the room as a particular group number or produce paper table cards or even yellow 'Post-It' stickers to slap onto appropriate walls.

I have spent a few moments describing the allocation to groups because a confident start to the workshop always works well. I often cringe when I'm taking part in a workshop only to find that the first 10 minutes are wasted by the workshop leader who cannot get organized. Also, if you are conducting a series of workshops there are advantages in changing group membership after several workshops. It may be an ideal opportunity for one participant to 'escape' from another – or make the acquaintance of someone in another group they have never met or worked with. Under the guise of sharing experiences and meeting new friends/escaping others, this is usually accepted.

Just one final thing about allocating numbers. I was once acutely embarrassed when I tried to allocate a participant to a group by gender – when I got the gender wrong! While eye contact is good for positive identification, a slightly glazed and searching scan of faces can sometimes avoid embarrassment.

Identification of participants

You may be conducting a workshop with people you already know and who know each other; if so there is little need for elaborate introductions. However, if some of the participants are unknown to others the use of name badges can be a real boon. Over the course of the workshop it creates a more personal and informal atmosphere if people are addressed by name. A few minutes at the beginning of a workshop asking participants to introduce themselves – who they are, where they are from, what they are doing, what they hope to get out of the workshop, etc. – can break the ice and contribute to the group atmosphere.

Just a brief word about name badges. Several types are available, from clear plastic holders that pin to clothing to the stick-on type. The beauty about the clear plastic ones is that they can be reused if collected. In most cases you are not being generous by letting people walk off with them because what invariably happens is that once out of the room the badges are thrown into the bin. The fabric, stick-on type are common, but typically they lose their 'stick' by the end of day two – and are not recommended for suede!

Workshop materials

The workshop booklet – key questions, discussion points, copies of overhead projector transparencies and selected references – represents the main resource you will need to conduct the workshop. However, you do need a few other things to help you record the comments, suggestions and ideas of participants.

When the group have discussed the question, topic or issue and the rapporteur has summarized the group's response you will need some way to share it with the rest of the group. You could always invite the rapporteur to '...share your group's comments and ideas with us', but you risk a lengthy monologue or worse some real insights which are lost because no one was able to write them down quickly enough.

It may sound obvious, but I would suggest that a clear way of recording group comments is both essential and beneficial.

One of the easiest ways is to give out sheets of paper from a flip chart – typically A0 size (841 mm × 1189 mm), felt-tipped pens and 'Blu-Tack'. The rapporteur can then summarize the group's comments on the paper, stick these to a convenient wall, window or door and talk through the points. It has the advantage that others can make notes about these comments and gives the rapporteur a teaching aid. Even the most competent people can often feel awkward when asked to summarize a group comment in public. The written summary can often be a useful aid. The only problem is that it is easy to get through a lot of paper if five groups create six sheets. Often the paper is of a quality that makes it impossible to turn over and use the reverse side because a ghost of the image shows through.

If you have an overhead projector you can simply distribute plain acetate sheets and felt-tipped pens. The rapporteur can simply summarize the group's comments and display them. If water-based pens are used you can even recycle the acetate. However, a note of warning. I would suggest that you use fine rather than medium felt-tipped pens because even the medium type gives a broad mark on the acetate, making the writing difficult to read or resulting in very few words and phrases per acetate sheet. Also, try to use the black, blue, red and green colours if possible; yellow and orange are difficult to read at a distance.

Of course, you may be one of the few workshop presenters who has access to an electronic whiteboard. This is a piece of equipment that looks like a conventional whiteboard upon which you can write as normal, but, when the board is full, the touch of a button will print an A4 copy of whatever was written on the screen; it will even run off multiple copies so that each participant can have one.

Timing

A magical mystery tour can be wonderful, but in my experience most workshop participants like to know where they are going, how they are going to get there and how long it will take. At various times I have been obliged to compress each of the following workshops into less than 30 minutes, and at other times have been invited to extend them to 3 hours. The optimum, I believe, is about 90 minutes. This is long enough to concentrate one's effort on a particular topic or series of questions, probably raising more questions than answers. It also means that one can conveniently fit two workshops into a morning or afternoon, with a mid-session break.

If you think this sounds rather leisurely then try it. I have been persuaded, against my better judgement, to fit three sessions into an afternoon and even mount an evening session. In practice I have found that concentration starts to wane after six hours, even with the most stimulating material. Also, the pace of the workshops is intended to be brisk. While it is possible to sustain this for four consecutive full sessions, participants have remarked that they become weary and irritable towards the end of the day – be warned.

Do try to stick to the time schedule you decide to adopt. Nothing irritates particip-ants more than laboured, pedestrian activities for most of the workshop and then a frantic scramble to finish only five minutes late! Similarly, nothing impresses par-ticipants more than concluding the last report-back as the teacups rattle outside the door – giving you the last two minutes to summarize, review or simply direct to se-lected references.

Comfort

It is worth giving some time and attention to the comfort of participants – especially if for most of the time they will be sitting down in a single room. You may, of course, have no control over the shape of chairs or the material from which covers are made, but if you have, exercise it. Would you like to sit on a solid plastic chair, perhaps in hot weather, for six hours? One more suitable for children or which drops you so far backwards that you have to 'sit forwards', doubled up, to hear what is being said in a group discussion? Participants may not thank you for the choice of chairs, worktops or tables – they may never even know – but the improved atmosphere and working conditions will be worth it.

Alerting participants about where to find toilets, telephones, fax machines, re-freshments and even banks and shops will not only answer possible questions but will reinforce the impression that you are organized and methodical. It is also worth finding out about the smoking policy in whatever institution you are working. Many offices, conference and meeting rooms are now non-smoking, so you may have no choice but to comply. Some have specially designated smoking areas to which you can direct participants. Of course, if no policy exists you can agree your own within the group. The most sensible may be to agree that the actual workshop room is non-smoking but that participants are free to leave at any time to smoke if they wish. (Morning, lunchtime and afternoon breaks should enable most particip-ants to smoke if they wish.)

One final point about comfort. Twenty or 30 people in a room, over a few hours, generate a lot of heat and consume a lot of oxygen. It may be a bit excessive to start a workshop by throwing open all the windows, but the sight of sleepy faces mid-morning or after lunch may be a cue for more ventilation.

Thanks

Finally, although it is customary to thank local staff, administrators and colleagues for initiating, publicizing and organizing the workshop, a personal letter to these people immediately after the event can bring disproportionate benefits – especially if you ever want to use the institution or facilities again.

Presentation of chapters – how the guidelines have been presented

A number of points need to be addressed prior to commencing the actual workshop. Indeed, you may be advised to allocate 10 minutes or so to various preliminaries:

- a brief welcome to the workshop and your introduction (2 minutes)
- allocating participants to small groups of 5–7 people (2 minutes)
- distribution of name tags and mutual introduction (if necessary) (5 minutes)
- distribution of workshop booklet and description of contents (1 minute).

Each workshop offers a short paragraph that can be the basis of a brief introduction or scene-setting statement for the workshop *and* a series of key questions. In subsequent pages a brief commentary is provided in relation to each question together with any appropriate quotes, examples, extracts or illustrations. A single summary, in the form of an OHT is given. Finally, several relevant references are offered.

The time you allocate to the whole workshop and to individual questions is obviously up to you. However, I would suggest you allocate at least five minutes to each question, since obtaining responses from groups of participants, via rapporteurs, and supplementing their comments with your own observations can easily consume a further 5 to 10 minutes per question. You can either call upon each of the rapporteurs in turn and begin building up a total summary of the area and then present your own ideas via the OHP or do it the other way round. Depending upon the quality of comments provided, the insights they offer and the time consumed, you can decide to invite each group to offer comments or restrict feedback to only some of them.

Needless to say, you will have to decide whether each of the questions offered is equally important to you and your participants. Do you want to delete any questions and replace them with others? Do you want to combine questions or substitute a brief observation of your own for participants' discussion of the question(s)? Whatever your method of personalizing the workshop it is likely that participants will thank you for a permanent record that they can annotate – to make it theirs. The sheets incorporating your opening statement and list of key questions, photocopies of the overhead projector transparencies you use, and copies of any quotes, extracts or examples you use will provide the basis of a permanent record.

Introduction – characteristics of self-instructional material

As a teacher, trainer, line manager or (whether you are aware of it or not) as a learner you will have used self-instructional material in open, distance or flexible learning contexts. In primary school it may have involved you giving children a work-card in arithmetic to complete, a tactile puzzle to solve or directions to follow in playing a game. In secondary school you may have provided directions to conduct an experiment, data to solve a problem or guidelines to undertake project work. In further education and training you may have prepared materials to simulate fault diagnosis or used multimedia and computer-based packages to provide a resource for your teaching. At its simplest you may have given learners a technical report, blueprint, circuit diagram or extract to study together with a series of questions to answer. You may have followed the manufacturer's instructions to assemble DIY furniture, programme the time control on the central heating or cooker – with different degrees of success! All of the above could constitute self-instructional material.

If you are involved in producing self-instructional material it would be worth considering what features of these materials you currently exploit. If you are planning to be involved you could consider what feature you could incorporate and thus maximize the effectiveness of your teaching. In doing so I would suggest that there are three key questions to address that relate to the first three chapters.

1. What are the distinctive features of self-instructional material?
2. What are the differences between textbooks and self-instructional material?
3. What are the differences between open, distance and flexible learning?

Chapter 1

Distinctive features of self-instructional material

The first paragraph in the Introduction above identifies several contexts in which self-instructional materials are used, whether in a financial/business, industrial/production or educational environment. Below I have reproduced the question, offered the example of *individual learning* and provided you with space in which to note those distinctive features you can identify.

1. What are the distinctive features of self-instructional material?
    *   Individual learning – no need to wait until there are enough learners to form a group.
    *
    *
    *
    *

You may be able to list several of these immediately. If not you could either talk to colleagues who use such materials and get their ideas; you could also inspect examples of materials your company, department or division currently uses. Whichever route you decide to follow, it is likely that once you start one feature will help to identify another.

Figure 1. 1 offers over a dozen features that many regard as distinctive features of self-instructional material; the figure summarizes the comments below. You can amend these to suit your situation.

Individual learning	No need to wait until there are enough learners to form a group.
Self-paced learning	Each individual can work at his or her own pace rather than at the pace of a group (which may be too fast or too slow).
Private learning	No danger of 'loss of face' as might be feared in certain kinds of group learning.
Available at any time	Learners can learn when they wish rather than according to an external timetable.
Available at any place	In students' homes or when travelling, unless fixed or special equipment is needed.
Available to any number	There is no limit to the number of learners who can be studying a course at one time.
Standardized content	All learners receive the same teaching materials.
Expert content	Materials can include contributions from national and international experts.
Updatable content	Package materials can usually be updated more quickly and cheaply than teachers.
Structured teaching	The teaching strategy can reflect a consensus of the most effective and efficient way to teach.
Active learning	Individuals learn by using ideas presented in the teaching rather than merely being told about them.
Frequent feedback	Learners should be getting continuous feedback to help them monitor and improve their own progress through the teaching package.
Explicit aims and objectives	It should be clear what learners might be expected to do as a result of working through the package.
Individualized tutoring	Tutors respond to individual learners' needs rather than repeating the teaching provided by the self-instructional materials.
Others	

Figure 1.1 *Distinctive features of self-instructional material*

1.1 Individual learning

A major and obvious feature of self-instructional material is that there is no need to wait until there are enough learners to form a viable group. Indeed, it is possible within a single group to have several programmes of study being followed. Those learners requiring additional or remedial help can have it provided at the same time as those who want additional practice or who wish to pursue their own special interests in an area. Needless to say, the self-instructional packages do not have to be lengthy nor limited to printed media and a home or teaching/training context. Brief video sequences dealing with, for example, fault diagnosis on a motor car braking system are available for use in the service area of garages. Mechanics can view the video, perform the required checks on the system, complete the fault diagnosis and effect a repair.

1.2 Self-paced learning

Each individual can work at his or her own pace rather than at the pace of the group – or rather the pace the teacher or trainer believes is the optimum! People do not study at a regular speed. Depending on their interests, background, personal experiences and other demands, students will complete their study of some material quickly; at other times it will take them longer. For example, all new Open University undergraduates were given preparatory materials to study prior to the start of their course. (The material was circulated in November prior to their course starting in February.) An evaluation revealed that one person studied these materials in 20 minutes while another took 180 hours! Forcing learners to progress at a pace too slow for them would be both frustrating and patronizing. However, if learners are forced to study too quickly it could be equally counter-productive. Leaving students 'trailing in your wake' is not to be recommended.

1.3 Private learning

How often have you been in a learning situation where you didn't understand some part of the explanation, procedure or technique? How often did you immediately put your hand up and advertise your ignorance – or did you keep quiet, hoping it would become clear or decide to check with fellow learners later? Self-instructional learning is private learning. Certainly, there is no 'loss of face' possible because there is no one else around to witness your confusion. However, it does put great emphasis on the need for clear teaching, with every opportunity for learners to monitor their progress, check their learning and resolve their problems.

In case the above comments suggest that private learning is 'second best' it should be mentioned that many learners actually say that they prefer to study on their own. Many of the students following the Hotel and Catering Course provided by the Hong Kong Polytechnic did so because they held senior positions and had considerable experience, but no formal qualifications. To attend a class with junior members of the industry was unthinkable. (Similar reasons have been expressed by UK managers!)

1.4 Available at any time

One of the main attractions of self-instructional material is that it is available at any time – when a learner wishes to study rather than according to some fixed timetable. Students not only study at different speeds, they also prefer to study at times convenient to themselves. The assumption that learners will study according to a regular, fixed schedule is a myth. The belief that regular broadcast transmissions or tutorials would 'pace' a student have been replaced by the realization that only assignment deadlines are likely to prompt study to a timetable. Indeed, we now realize that between such assignment deadlines study is likely to be irregular for the majority of students. Students pace themselves according to their own schedule and competing demands.

Where a course follows a linear sequence it is common for students to 'fall behind' and then undertake a period of intensive study to 'catch up' or 'get ahead'. Where courses resemble a resource, with the ability to study in virtually any sequence, it is common for learners to focus on what they either find most interesting or what they need immediately. For example, an explanation of the appropriateness of different statistical procedures and how to conduct them may be needed now rather than in several weeks' time.

1.5 Available at any place

A distinctive feature of self-instructional material is that it is available at any place: in students' homes, when travelling, at the workplace or on holiday! The only limitation would be where some audio, video, practical work or computer-based materials are needed. However, at the present time and for the immediate future the majority of self-instructional materials are likely to be based on print and are thus portable, cheap and flexible. What is more, audio, video and other components are typically flagged in the text, allowing learners to arrange their study so that any necessary equipment or facilities are available when required.

Many learners describe how they fit their study around their lives – studying between breakfast and going to work, during the lunch break and on the bus home. Indeed, one student, a bus driver, described how he completed a degree while sitting in the cab of his bus prior to and at the end of his bus route journey. Furthermore, many teachers and trainers have acknowledged that simple 'kitchen sink experiments', using everyday items, can be used to illustrate the principles and relationships that have previously required laboratories, workshops or clinical settings. Portable cassette tape recorders, and more recently laptop microcomputers, allow multimedia self-instructional material to be studied virtually anywhere.

1.6 Available to any number

In principle there is no limit to the number of learners who can study a course at any one time. Above, I mentioned the problem often encountered by conventional institutions of requiring a viable sized group; sometimes the reverse is true! For example, when the British police force wished to inform its officers of changes to the British Road Traffic Act, 1991, it was faced with the problem of informing over 80,000 officers as soon as possible. It was considered impractical to provide conventional face-to-face training; it would simply take too long for small groups to attend particular training venues while maintaining adequate active staffing levels. The solution was to assemble a self-instructional booklet and make this instantly available to all officers.

Facilities for rapid duplication of printed material and audio and video tapes, plus economies of scale, make self-instructional material for large groups particularly attractive.

1.7 Standardized content

Learners deserve the best teaching and training materials that we can provide; materials that are not adversely affected by the particular preferences or idiosyncrasies of a teacher or trainer. A feature of self-instructional material is that it enables all learners to receive the same teaching material. Furthermore, since the materials are available for scrutiny by others it is likely that current thinking and the accepted arguments are likely to be central – rather than the personal views of the author.

In large institutions it is not unusual for a group of learners to be taught by two or more teachers/trainers – each following the same syllabus or scheme of work. However, often an independent observer would be excused if they judged that two completely different courses were being taught! Indeed, even when one person is responsible for the teaching, and conducts duplicate classes, the difference between the presentations is likely to be significant.

1.8 Expert content

You may, or may not, be the world expert in your field. However, a distinctive feature of self-instructional material is that you can include contributions in your teaching from colleagues as well as national and international experts. An obvious way is to include existing published material in your teaching – particular articles, extracts, pamphlets, technical reports, etc (ensuring you do not infringe copyright). These may represent a degree of detail and quality of writing that you are unable to improve upon. You may be able to persuade them to record an audio tape – perhaps a discussion with you or a debate with another colleague. Depending on the resources and technical expertise available you may even be able to take the learners to places they would find impossible to visit by recording such situations, events, techniques or whatever on videotape. Your learners may be able to take part in online discussion with an expert or other learners via a computer-mediated communication (CMC) link.

Of course, you do not have to automatically agree completely with the arguments, positions and theories of models put forward by these 'experts'. Indeed, you may wish to compare and contrast these views – presenting them to the learners and inviting them to make up their own minds.

1.9 Updatable content

The upgrading of teachers and trainers is typically a costly and time-consuming task, even when they acknowledge a need for retraining. Furthermore, while the initial impact of in-service training may be substantial, teachers and trainers often fail to implement all the previously acknowledged good practice. For example, at the end of a course designed to improve the teaching of literacy among schoolchildren the value of new methods was recognized. However, subsequent checks revealed that teachers gradually reverted to previously acknowledged inferior practices as time progressed.

In contrast, self-instructional materials are cheap and quick to update. The availability of desktop publishing techniques means that printed materials can be revised rapidly. Furthermore, on-demand printing means that documents can be reproduced in minutes. For example, high-speed laser photocopiers are able to print and bind a 48 page A4 booklet, including high-quality photographs, at a rate of one every two minutes. The integration of colour photocopies is also possible. This, together with high-speed audio and video copying, means that once the desired changes have been made to originals, copies can be generated overnight. World-Wide Web pages can be created virtually as fast as you can type.

1.10 Structured teaching

If you asked a dozen subject matter specialists, independently, to design a particular package to satisfy an agreed aim and series of objectives you would probably get a dozen different ways of doing it. Some would take longer than others to study, some would stress one element rather than another, and some would consume more resources than others. The structure of the packages and sequence of elements would undoubtedly vary. Of course, in reality many teachers and trainers are only required to provide the briefest of outlines for a particular programme of study. It is often merely a list of topics or lecture titles supplemented by two or three sentences. What is more, a detailed description or overview of the course, let alone individual modules or study sessions, is typically provided in a paragraph in course publicity material.

A distinctive feature of self-instructional material is that the teaching structure and sequence is made explicit. Preliminary documents, often an Introduction and Guide, provide the general structure of the course, while preliminary pages in each module indicate the structure and sequence of the teaching material – and alternative ways through it. If the material is assembled by two or more authors, or they have the advice and assistance of others, they can devise a teaching strategy that reflects a consensus of the most effective and efficient way to teach the topic.

1.11 Active learning

In higher education, and much of further education, the lecture is still widely held as an obvious method of conveying information. The problem is that the teacher does all the work – all the telling. The learner is reduced to the role of one who must merely comprehend, interpret and remember; often little opportunity is provided to ask questions, resolve misunderstandings or clarify ideas. Unfortunately, many learners still appear to believe that this method has merit until given the opportunity to experience an alternative way of studying.

A distinctive feature of self-instructional material is that individuals learn by using ideas presented in the teaching material rather than merely being told about them. The provision of exercises, activities or self-assessment questions is the mechanism by which the key objectives associated with a teaching text are realized and students allowed to practise them.

It is sobering to learn that when two modules of a course were compared by students, one containing activities and one in which none were present, the majority of students said the absence of activities hindered their learning (Duchastel and Whitehead, 1980).

1.12 Frequent feedback

A knowledge of one's performance, the appropriateness of one's response to questions, confirmation of ideas and relationships (or their refutation) are at the core of learning. All teachers and trainers would seek to provide feedback to students on their learning. Unfortunately, many lectures, seminars and even workplace forms of teaching fail to provide adequate feedback. A distinctive feature of self-instructional material is that learners receive continuous feedback to help them monitor their learning and check on their performance as they progress through the teaching package.

Traditionally, the feedback is provided in periodic comments to learners in response to tests, quizzes or assignments. A critical factor is not merely the quality of the original questions and corresponding feedback, but the speed with which it is provided. If a considerable amount of time elapses between posing the problem(s), encouraging a response and providing feedback, its efficiency is in doubt. Learners' misunderstandings may have been reinforced or unnecessary confusion allowed to continue. Self-instructional material is designed to provide the feedback continuously – essentially via the self-assessment questions or activities integrated into the text, the CD-ROM or Web pages, but also by the quality of the exposition. In many situations the feedback provided by teachers and trainers is designed to indicate the scope and depth of preferred responses; to indicate the quality expected of learners at a particular stage. For example, when OU staff wanted to indicate the scope and depth of forthcoming assignments in technology they gave students the opportunity to complete a mini-assignment *before* the start of the course. At the same time they were provided with examples of three typical assignment attempts, corresponding to a good, an average and a poor response. The subsequent evaluation indicated that students were able to judge the adequacy of their attempt and what they would need to do to improve or maintain the grade they awarded themselves.

1.13 Explicit aims and objectives

As an experienced teacher or trainer, when faced with a particular topic to teach to a group of learners, you would typically decide how you intended to teach it and what you expected learners to be able to do at the end of your teaching; you would formulate the aims and objectives of the lesson. While many teachers and trainers convey these to their learners, and even have them as written statements (as in NVQs), it is not unusual for general goals to be listed in some course outline and for statements of objectives to be absent or 'implicit' in the teaching.

A distinctive feature of self-instructional materials is that they contain explicit aims and objectives – clear statements as to what the teacher is planning to do and what learners are supposed to be able to do after completing their study. Indeed, many self-instructional materials not only specify the objectives but indicate the place(s) in the material where they are achieved. The *house style* of the teaching material is often such that aims and objectives are always provided at particular points in the teaching material so that learners can refer readily to them.

1.14 Individualized tutoring

How can a distinctive feature of self-instructional material be individualized tutoring? Surely this is a feature of conventional teaching! If self-instructional teaching material is supported by a tutor then such a person is able to respond to the individual learner's needs in response to specific questions – be they by telephone, fax, email or face-to-face meetings. If a course of study has assignments a tutor is able to provide comments on the script(s) – either by writing typed messages via email or by talking the student through the points on audio tape. Several institutions, such as Monash University in Australia, the Open University of the Netherlands and the Open University in the UK offer courses where students submit assignments or complete examinations online – with greatly improved turn round of grades and comments to learners.

Many would argue that in assembling self-instructional material the teacher should be trying to simulate the ideal tutorial relationship and *talking* to the learners – drawing upon their experience, posing questions, anticipating problems, directing to other sources, etc.

1.15 Others

The above list is illustrative, not exhaustive. It is likely that other distinctive features will occur to you or emerge from the particular learning environment in which you work. The key point is not which are most important and should be higher in the hierarchy, but that they reflect your self-instructional material.

Reference

Duchastel, P S and Whitehead, D (1980) Exploring student reactions to inserted questions in texts, *Programme Learning and Educational Technology*, **17**(1), 41–7.

Chapter 2

Differences between textbooks and self-instructional material

In the Introduction I said that whether you were aware of it or not I suspect that you will have used self-instructional material in open, distance or flexible learning contexts. However, I suspect that you may be more familiar with writing technical reports, textbooks, book chapters, academic articles, etc. than self-instructional material. Indeed, I also suspect that you are very much aware that you typically adopt a particular style, format and language for the various documents you do write. But how do the style, format and language of a typical textbook differ from typical self-instructional material? If you are aware of these differences you will be more able to exploit them in your teaching or training materials. Below I have reproduced the question, offered the example of 'interest in the material' and provided you with space in which to note those differences you can identify.

2. What are the differences between textbooks and self-instructional material?
    -   Textbooks assume interest – self-instructional material arouses interest.

    -

    -

    -

    -

In the example I suggest that a typical textbook is likely to assume that the purchaser or reader is interested in the subject matter – if not, why else would that person buy it or sit down to read it? In contrast I would suggest that the typical self-instructional material should try to arouse interest. You will not be at the learner's shoulder all the time – encouraging, prompting, questioning, clarifying and indicating the relevance of the material.

So what are the differences between a typical textbook and typical self-instructional material? Again, you can either try to identify these yourself in three or four minutes or pool ideas with your colleagues. Figure 2.1 summarizes some of the differences that others have noted, and the text below elaborates. However, I should say that in making the distinction between a typical book and typical self-instructional material I have focused on the extreme characteristics. Not all textbooks are poor and display all these features. Similarly, not all self-instructional materials are good and embody all the attractive features listed. You may agree or disagree with some of these differences and add others. In doing so I hope it highlights many of the characteristics of these materials and their implications for you and your learners.

Textbooks	Self-instructional materials
Assumes interest	Arouses interest
Written for teacher use	Written for learner use
No indication of study time	Gives estimates of study time
Designed for a wide market	Designed for a particular audience
Rarely state aims and objectives	Always gives aims and objectives
Usually one route through	May be many ways through it
Structured for specialists	Structured according to needs of learner
Little or no self-assessment	Major emphasis on self-assessment
Seldom anticipates difficulties	Alert to potential difficulties
Occasionally offers summaries	Always offers summaries
Impersonal style	Personal style
Dense content	Content unpacked
Dense layout	More open layout
Readers views seldom sought	Learner evaluation always conducted
No study skills advice	Provides study skills advice
Can be read passively	Requires active response
Aims at scholarly presentation	Aims at successful teaching
Others	

Figure 2.1 *Some differences between textbooks and self-instructional material*

2.1 Written for teacher use/written for learner use

Textbooks are typically written for teachers and trainers, not learners. How often have you given learners a *whole* book to read, handing over the responsibility for your teaching to that author? I suspect not very often. However, like me, I suspect you have directed learners to a particular chapter or section with some guidance as to why the extract is important, why it is worth reading, how it links to other teaching, the purpose behind getting them to study it, etc. I also suspect, like me, that you have summarized the preceding text or told learners not to read further – often because to do so would raise more problems than answers, because the learners are not adequately prepared for the ideas and arguments, that they will not understand the terminology, that they wouldn't be prepared for the subsequent issues or whatever. It really is extremely common for teachers and trainers to mediate the books that they use to maximize their teaching.

In contrast, self-instructional materials, by definition, have to be written for learner use. You will be giving your learners a collection of materials (which may include published material) from which you expect them to study, often for hours. The purpose behind their study and specific directions must be clear. The material must be pitched at the appropriate level and the language must be at an appropriate level. You really do want to be sure that every learner has every chance of completing their study successfully.

2.2 No indication of study time/gives estimate of study time

When was the last time you picked up a textbook and it gave an indication of how long it would take you to study a particular chapter? It doesn't happen very often and the reasons are fairly obvious. While the author may have a particular audience in mind, it is impossible to know precisely who will be reading it – their previous knowledge, experience, interest, etc. Different readers are likely to be seeking different things from the text, and as such it is extremely difficult, if not impossible, to estimate how long it would take to study. However, if you are incorporating some existing published material in your teaching I assume you would be doing so with a clear purpose. With your knowledge of your learners, and what you are wanting them to do, it is not unreasonable to expect that you would indicate how long the text would take to study for them to gain from it what you intended.

I would hope that the last time you picked up some self-instructional material it did give an indication of how long it would take to study. In fact, I would go further and hope that all the main components of the material – be they exercises, texts to study, tapes to view or listen to, or projects and assignments to complete – would be accompanied by an indication of study time. Certainly, where institutions are charging learners for the course of study, they are increasingly aware that they are entering a contract with their learners. Part of this contract is typically an indication of how long a learner will be expected to commit to the course per week (or session) in order to be able to satisfy course demands.

All the evidence indicates that extremely few students study in a regular, unchanging schedule. Work, domestic and social commitments all have to be fitted around their study – or rather the study has to be fitted around their other commitments. In planning their work it is thus vital that students have an indication of how long a particular experiment, exercise, computer simulation or text to study is likely to take.

2.3 Designed for a wide market/designed for a particular audience

If you have ever assembled a book proposal, or negotiated a proposal with a publisher, you will be aware of their desire to maximize sales by appealing to as wide an audience as possible. The range of the desired audience may not extend from schoolchildren to Nobel prizewinners, but the problems caused by trying to satisfy a wide audience remain. The terminology used may be in common use or intimidating, or the level at which the arguments are discussed may be facile or at a degree of detail that is inappropriate. The examples and illustrations may be valuable in one country or context but divorced from another reader's comprehension.

In contrast, I believe that your self-instructional material needs to be designed for a specific audience – your particular learners. The material will acknowledge their previous learning, be pitched at an appropriate level, contain appropriate examples and exercises, and satisfy their particular needs at that period in time. (In Chapter 3 we shall consider what you know about your learners and what you may wish to know.)

2.4 Rarely state aims and objectives/always gives aims and objectives

When was the last time you opened a textbook and it clearly specified the author's aim and the objectives you would be able to achieve? Until a few years ago I suspect you would have said none, or that they were buried in the text. However, things are changing, and an increasing number of books are becoming available that do give the reader an indication of what is intended and what the reader can expect.

The problem, of course, relates to the preceding point. If the book is trying to satisfy a wide audience, the inevitable possibility is that different readers will be seeking different things and the book will allow a whole variety and range of objectives to be achieved. One way in which this is happening is by the co-publication of course materials. Core materials are assembled and supplemented by different study guides, with each study guide presenting different populations of learners with different aims and objectives. In this way, the same basic resource can be used for different audiences. However, unlike the typical textbook, self-instructional materials should always give clear indications of their aims and objectives (see 'Explicit aims and objectives', page 8).

2.5 Usually one route through/may be many ways through it

In the typical textbook there is normally one route through it; you start at the beginning and work through to the end. The author develops the arguments, refines the techniques and reveals increasingly complex procedures or applications; the story is gradually told. Often the effect of the material in the text is cumulative, with one chapter building on another and subsequent chapters only making sense if the preceding points have been explained. This is why, when directing learners to an isolated chapter of a book, you summarize the preceding material and often advise them not to read on. However, our lives are full of examples where we do not read everything from page one to the end. We don't read a newspaper, mail order catalogue or telephone directory in this way. When reprogramming the time switch on the cooker we turn directly to that section of the instruction manual that explains how to do it. In many examples of teaching material there are often different places where learners can commence their study and many routes through it. Some years ago, around the time of programmed text and teaching machines, scrambled texts were popular. Depending on the response you gave to a particular question, the text directed you to certain pages – it was impossible to simply read the book from page one. You may even have been fortunate to read the book by Robert Mager, *Preparing Instructional Objectives* (Mager, 1990), which adopted this approach.

Depending on the interests, needs, abilities and time available to your learners, they may follow different routes through your teaching material. Earlier, in comments on Self-paced learning (see page 4), I mentioned that in the Open University preparatory material for the Technology Foundation course there was a wide range in the amount of time students committed to it. What I didn't mention was that learners had a degree of choice as to the route(s) they followed through the material. Figure 2.2 is a copy of the diagram that was presented to these students and which they were talked through to help them decide which route they wanted to follow. After Section 1, would they turn immediately to Technological issues in Section 7 and study material of a type typical of that they would meet in the course? After working though Section 3, Thinking about preparation, would they follow route C, assess their numeracy skills and concentrate upon Block 1, Numeracy tributary, or route D and assess their literacy skills and consult the text Plain English? You will not be standing by the learners' shoulders, ensuring they follow your suggested route. As such it may be wise to alert learners to the different possibilities and to know that there is nothing wrong in different routes to the same goal.

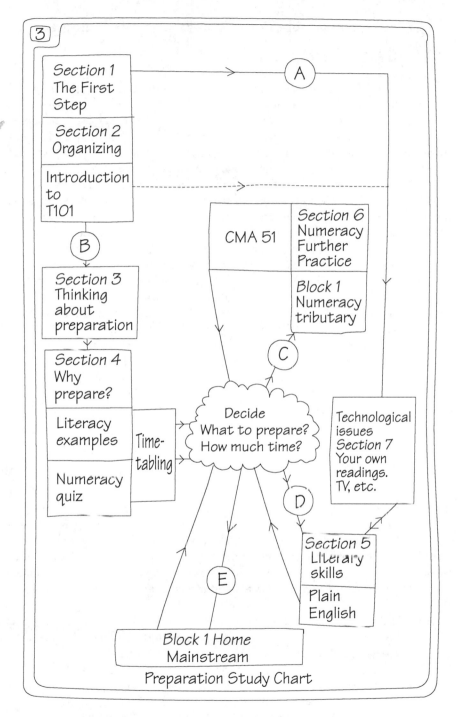

Figure 2.2 *Diagram that learners are 'talked through' when considering how to prepare for study*

2.6 Structured for specialists/structured according to needs of learner

Writing a book isn't easy – ask any author. Often it is the culmination of lengthy research and/or years of practice and experience, with the author wanting to make a contribution to his or her field and to share new ideas, perspectives, interpretations, models or theories. If it wasn't new, innovative or offering something different there would be little call for its publication! In such circumstances it is common for such texts to be written for colleagues in the field – for other specialists. In such situations the author is unlikely to recount, in painstaking detail, all the academic background to the book, previous practices, trends or beliefs, but merely to refer the initiated to them and to concentrate on the new ideas, perspectives, etc. Often the field will have evolved a hierarchy or matrix of categories, accepted stages, particular lines of argument or positions. Textbooks typical emerge from, contribute to, and extend a particular body of knowledge – they are structured for specialists.

Unfortunately, most learners are not in such a privileged position; they do not have the benefit of extensive research insights or background in the area. The common knowledge shared by specialists may be unknown to learners and needs to be taught, not merely recounted. Furthermore, even when teachers consciously structure materials for learners and offer this structure as the optimum route, there is no guarantee that students will accept it. When an optimum study route was offered to learners studying a Materials Science course, only a quarter followed it; the majority decided to 'find their own route'.

2.7 Little or no self-assessment/major emphasis on self-assessment

Textbooks are typically strong on exposition and weak on questioning. The points in the text are presented with the author providing the required examples and comparisons, indicating any inconsistencies, identifying implications and drawing any conclusions. The author does all the work and all the telling, and as such there is little or no self-assessment unless it is provided by others. When questions are incorporated they are typically grouped at the end of a chapter or section, often with no feedback.

A major difference between typical textbooks and self-instructional material is the sheer volume of self-assessment material in the latter; it really is a characteristic feature. When examples or comparisons are needed the learner is invited to offer them. The learner can be challenged to identify inconsistencies, possible applications of the idea, techniques or whatever. Students are encouraged to check their understanding and competence through their completion of the self-assessment activities – to realize the course objectives.

2.8 Seldom anticipates difficulties/alert to potential difficulties

A textbook is typically as refined, balanced and complete as the author is able to make it. There are typically no 'loose ends', no incomplete analyses, no remaining confusion – merely areas for further investigation and consideration. Indeed, the trigger for many authors is that after considerable effort the problem, issue or solution is suddenly clear. The colleagues who suddenly make announcements like 'it suddenly all falls into place... the model is so elegant... the theory so pervasive... the solution feasible' do so after considerable time working on the topic and often with considerable previous academic or technical experience. The message that is conveyed to peers may acknowledge the difficulties that faced the author, but seldom, if ever, suggests that the reader will have difficulty in understanding the text – because it is as 'refined, balanced and complete as the author is able to make it'.

Teachers and trainers typically anticipate the problems that are likely to arise. Alternative explanations are prepared, additional exercises are assembled and examples are provided. In conventional teaching situations the raised hand, puzzled expression or deathly quiet upon posing a question immediately flag a problem. Learners studying self-instructional texts may not have someone readily available to respond to their questions – the problematic areas need to be anticipated and material taught.

2.9 Occasionally offers summaries/always offers summaries

While virtually all books contain a concluding chapter, not all contain chapter summaries. Not all authors follow the practice (attributed to the military, but often employed by teachers and trainers) of 'telling them what you are going to tell them, telling them, and telling them of what you have told them'. Indeed, one can understand authors who are experts in the topic area, and believe that they have done all they can to explain, describe and illustrate the material that constitutes the book, who feel that summaries are mere duplication of what has already been said. Unfortunately, the readers of such books may not always be the peers of the author, and a restatement of the previous ideas, arguments or whatever may offer valuable reinforcement.

Self-instructional materials typically have concluding sections – they should always have part or section summaries. Of course, these summaries do not have to be in the form of a short paragraph of text. A diagrammatic representation or concept map can often encapsulate the main ideas and the links or relationships between them. Photographs of 'before', 'during' and 'after' can summarize the key stages or phases of an action, be it a golf swing or the pruning of fruit trees. An annotated 'good' example can flag the main aspects of a task or provide an *aide-mémoire* – such as the elements of a corrected laid-out letter or financial balance sheet.

2.10 Impersonal style/personal style

If you were delivering a formal lecture, say at some professional gathering or at a conference, I suspect you would adopt a particular tone, talk at a certain speed and use particular language. I suspect these would be very different if you were discussing a technical or academic point with your immediate colleagues or talking as part of your teaching in a lesson, tutorial or practical session with learners. We use different styles of language in different contexts. Similarly, authors adopt a particular style when writing a book, academic paper or technical report. It is impersonal, detached and typified by the use the third person – speaking of 'the author', 'the reader' or 'the client'. It is also characterized by long sentences with numerous and varied clauses. It is a style that has evolved over hundreds of years and to which authors readily conform.

Of course, just as you adopt a different spoken style in different contexts it is possible to adopt a different writing style – one that is close to the tone, speed and language that you would use with learners. When writing self-instructional material it is possible to adopt a tone that is more personal, a speed that is slower and more relaxed, and a language that is closer to everyday conversation. I have deliberately tried to adopt such a style in this book, to resist supporting every claim with a reference and to avoid the academic practice of justifying every statement in terms of the theoretical model or academic framework from which it emerges. You will also note that I have used short simple sentences and the first person throughout, talking of you, I, we and them. I trust you have found the style more personal and engaging, while still conveying the key information.

2.11 Dense content/content unpacked

A feature of academic writing is its economy in exposition; message(s) are conveyed succinctly with minimum redundancy. Authors typically assume readers' familiarity with the academic or technical area and as such there is no need to recount the details of every theory, model, technique or whatever to which they have alluded. For their audience it is sufficient merely to name the theory, mention the model and refer to the technique, perhaps with a supporting academic or technical reference. The focus of the book is typically on the new ideas, interpretations, variations, treatment or whatever that makes the book a contribution to the field.

In contrast, self-instructional material constitutes a teaching document. Previous teaching may have outlined a particular theory, model or technique with the current intention to develop them. However, if this previous teaching cannot be assumed it may be necessary to provide material that not all learners will need; to build in some redundancy. Depending on the judgement of the author and knowledge of the learner audience this may be in appendices or in the main body of the teaching material. Similar judgements may be needed as to the sequence of ideas to be presented, with the opportunity for learners to focus on some elements and skip over others.

2.12 Dense layout/more open layout

In assembling a book proposal, and negotiating it with a publisher, the author is often placed in a dilemma regarding the things that he or she wants to say, how to say it and the space available. Your book proposal may suggest such things as number of words; page size; number of photographs, diagrams and figures; and use of colour. It may even suggest that it is published in paperback rather than hardback. However, the publishing world is as competitive as any other. When it comes to the costing of a book these elements, together with the type and size of font, paper quality and the key decision over the print run, are critical to the cost of the book and how it will fit into the existing list of titles. These decisions are invariably made by the publisher. The resulting contract stipulates the number of words, number of tables, etc. because the cover price of the book will have been decided on all of the above variables. The number of words is often reduced, and the desire to 'say what needs to be said', together with some of the points listed so far, often results in a dense layout.

Teaching and training organizations tend not to incur the sort of publishing, publicity and distribution costs that publishing houses have to carry. The house style is often set, and although each additional page, figure and table does incur a cost, it is likely to be relatively small compared with the staff costs of actually producing the academic or technical content. The inclusion of advance organizers, like aims and objectives, and diagrammatic representations of the structure, together with space for activities, all contribute to a more open layout. White space is used to maximum effect.

2.13 Readers' views seldom sought/learner evaluation always conducted

It is usual for authors to acknowledge the help and support of colleagues in assembling a book. But how often, in the various textbooks you have studied or written, have the readers' views been sought? Martin Tessmer, in his book *Planning and Conducting Formative Evaluations* (Tessmer, 1993), actually included a paragraph in the preliminary pages explaining 'How this book was formatively evaluated'; it included expert review and field test evaluation with learners. Derek Rowntree, in an introduction to his book *Exploring Open and Distance Learning* (Rowntree, 1992), remarked:

> If you feel like writing to tell me how you got on with this book, I'll be very pleased to hear from you. In particular, I would be interested to hear how the book might help in your professional work and how you think it might be improved for the benefit of future readers.

However, formative evaluations and seeking of readers views are not common. The evaluation of self-instructional material is much more common, so as to improve it for future learners. During course production it may involve expert review and developmental testing (Zand, 1994). During course presentation it may involve an evaluation of *all* course components, from administrative arrangements and the study material to learner support and assessment. Indeed, a colleague who has been involved in course evaluations for many years (Calder, 1994) argues that those involved in open and distance education should be working towards the goal of being self-improving organizations.

2.14 No study skills advice/provides study skills advice

In an earlier section I mentioned that you read newspapers, mail order catalogues and self-instructional material in different ways; you employ various reading strategies as part of your repertoire of study skills. A sobering question is to ask 'who provided you with study skills advice about learning from text, diagrams, charts... audio, video and computer based materials?' Whenever I have posed this question to colleagues the majority have said they simply 'picked it up'. While these colleagues are fortunate, and the successful ones, what about those who are unlucky and don't 'pick it up'? Certainly, authorities like Tony Bates (Bates, 1995) and Graham Gibbs (Gibbs, 1981) maintain that the skills needed to learn from different media are not simple and unproblematic. A large proportion of textbooks assume that readers have already acquired the study skills they need to benefit most from the text; this is a big assumption.

Many teachers and trainers assembling self-instructional material acknowledge that their learners need advice on study skills. Large organizations like the Open University, National Extension College and Open College have published excellent books to meet this need (Northedge, 1990; Freeman and Mead, 1990; Good, 1990). The section on self-paced learning mentioned the preparatory materials that were given to Open University students prior to their commencement of the course. Others have provided study skills advice at appropriate points in the teaching material.

2.15 Can be read passively/requires active response

Earlier, in the section on 'Little or no self-assessment/major emphasis on self-assessment', I said:

> Textbooks are typically strong on exposition and weak on questioning. The points in the text are presented with the author providing the required examples and comparisons, indicating any inconsistencies, identifying implications and drawing any conclusions. The author does all the work, all the telling.

The result is that books can be in danger of doing all the thinking for the learner; the only task is to read and comprehend. The learner is able to read the material passively with the expectation that in the next paragraph or page the solution to the problem or alternatives will be presented.

Because self-instructional materials place a major emphasis on self-assessment they require an active response. Indeed, it is not unusual for authors to begin drafting their self-instructional teaching material by designing the self-assessment questions or activities that will be the core of their teaching; that realize the key objectives. If the activities give good reasons why they are worth completing, clear instructions and a framework for a response, the chances of students being actively involved is high (Lockwood, 1992).

2.16 Aims at scholarly presentation/aims at successful teaching

I suspect that you will have spotted a slight change in my writing style in the last page or so – a sudden increase in the academic references given with the suggestion that other authorities will support the points I am making – if you took the time to locate the books and read them. When writing textbooks, these, together with an impersonal style and an economy of exposition which is pitched to the level of peers, are some of the features of scholarly presentation. Unfortunately for learners, such scholarly presentations are more likely to intimidate and alienate than invite and encourage.

Self-instructional materials aim at successful teaching where the audience are the learners *not* other teachers and trainers. However, unlike a conventional teaching situation, where the workshop, laboratory or seminar room contains everyone who will witness the teaching, self-instructional materials readily become public property; they are often privately and publicly reviewed by colleagues. A danger is for authors to 'look over their shoulder' towards their peers and to try to impress them with their scholarship rather than satisfy the teaching needs of their learners. Academic references are important and so are the type of exposition and level at which the material is pitched. However, it is seldom necessary to study every paragraph with references or to imply an explanation merely by mention of them.

2.17 Others

You will undoubtedly be able to identify other differences between textbooks and self-instructional material. I would also be surprised if you accepted all of the above without question. However, I trust the exercise and comments have alerted you to some of the differences and the pitfalls to avoid.

References

Bates, A (1995) *Technology, Open Learning and Distance Education*, Routledge, London.

Calder, J (1994) *Programme Evaluation and Quality,* Kogan Page, London.

Freeman, R and Mead, J (1990) *How to Study Effectively*, National Extension College, Cambridge.

Gibbs, G (1981) *Teaching Students to Learn: A Student-Centred Approach,* Open University Press, Milton Keynes.

Good, M (1990) *The Effective Learner*, The Open College, London.

Lockwood, F G (1992) *Activities in Self-Instructional Texts*, Kogan Page, London.

Mager, R (1990) *Preparing Instructional Objectives*, Kogan Page, London.

Northedge, A *The Good Study Guide*, Open University Press, Milton Keynes.

Rowntree, D (1992) *Exploring Open and Distance Learning,* Kogan Page, London.

Tessmer, M (1993) *Planning and Conducting Formative Evaluation*, Kogan Page, London.

Zand, H (1994) Developmental testing: monitoring academic quality and teaching, in *Materials Production in Open and Distance Learning* (ed F Lockwood), Paul Chapman Publishing, London.

Chapter 3

Differences between open, distance and flexible learning

You may have a clear picture as to what constitutes open, distance and flexible learning, and be able to define these terms and explain the differences between them. If this is the case, you could always note your definitions and observations in the space below before reading on.

3. What are the differences between open, distance and flexible learning? (How would you define these terms?)

- Open learning

- Distance learning

- Flexible learning

- Main differences between them.

However, let me assume that you are not completely confident about your ability to do this, are not working on your own and feel it would be worthwhile sharing your ideas with others and establishing some common definitions with your colleagues. From the same starting point, here are two simple ways to make progress and formulate a working definition of open learning.

3.1 Open learning

Personal definitions

As a starting point you need to ask each person to write a definition of the three terms, starting with open learning, each on a separate slip of paper.

The easiest way to do this is to provide colleagues with the three terms as separate headings, equally spaced, on one side of A5 paper (Figure 3.1).

Open learning
Distance learning
Flexible learning

Figure 3.1 *Personal definitions of terms*

The people involved can be given two minutes to draft a definition for the first term. At the end of this time they simply rip off the slip of paper and put it to one side before drafting the next definition. This has the advantage that those writing definitions do not have much space or time in which to note the main features; no one is expecting perfect definitions.

Alternative A – comparison with existing definitions

Any brief review of books in the field will provide existing definitions. For the purpose of the exercise it is perfectly acceptable to copy several different definitions, to paste them onto separate index cards and to provide these to your group(s) of colleagues. The group task is then to identify a rapporteur (someone who will make a note of the discussion and summarize their conclusions) and then to:

- review these existing definitions
- identify the key elements
- compare with personal definitions
- agree a working definition.

You may have particular definitions that you would want to present to your colleagues, definitions that include or stress particular features. In Figure 3.2 I offer several definitions of open learning which I believe present the most common features.

An open learning system is one which enables individuals to take part in programmes of studies of their choice, no matter where they live or whatever their circumstances.

Council for Educational Technology (1980, page 8)

...arrangements to enable people to learn at the time, place, and pace which satisfies their circumstances and requirements. The emphasis is on opening up opportunities by overcoming barriers that result from geographical isolation, personal or work commitments or conventional course structures which have often prevented people from gaining access to the training they need.

Manpower Services Commission (1984, page 7)

- accommodate directly the ways in which people learn naturally
- open up various choices and degrees of control to learners
- be based on learning materials which are learner-centred
- help learners to take credit for their learning, and develop a positive feeling of ownership of their success
- help conserve human skills for things that really need human presence and feedback.

Race (1994, page 29)

1. Study wherever it is convenient, whether at home or work.
2. Enrol at any time, without having to worry about previous qualifications.
3. Study at a pace which suits the learner.
4. Leave the system in a manner which suits the learner.
5. Have access at his or her own discretion to tutorial support and guidance.

Webberley and Haffenden (1987, page 138)

Figure 3.2 *Definitions of open learning*

Alternative B – reaching a group consensus

If you have a small group of colleagues an alternative approach would be to form them into a group and get them to reach a group consensus over the key elements they wish to see reflected in a definition and to work towards it.

A pair of colleagues could be given the personal definitions of open learning from two other colleagues. Their task, in say five minutes, is then to:

- review these personal definitions
- identify the key elements
- agree a working definition.

At the end of the time period you can combine groups and give the new group another five minutes to pool their suggestions and agree a revised definition. You can decide whether to present the published definitions and form a final definition or adopt the revised one.

3.2 Key elements

Depending on the personal and published definitions you assemble you will be able to identify a variety of features. The definition from the Manpower Services Commission (MSC) in Figure 3.2 typifies the common feature of overcoming barriers to learning. Below I comment on some of the key elements.

Geographical location

If learners physically cannot get to the place where the course if offered, if it takes too much time to get there or if travel costs too much, it doesn't matter how good the course may be – they still cannot benefit from it.

The Society of Cosmetic Scientists runs a successful course in Cosmetic Science at the London College of Fashion. Unfortunately, it is only open to the 18–20 people who could travel to London every Monday to Friday evening, during term time, to attend the programme of lectures. By transforming the course into a self-instructional course, learners all over the world were able to study it. In its first year it attracted 75 students, with a third of these outside the UK (Lockwood and Lewis, 1994).

Personal and work commitments

Contrary to the belief of many teachers and trainers, learners – even school-aged learners – have personal and work commitments. You may expect school-aged learners to study most evenings and at the weekend and even over holidays – unfortunately leisure, social and domestic commitments during the week and paid employment at weekends can consume large amounts of time. The personal, social and work commitments of adults are likely to be even more demanding.

When the Hong Kong Polytechnic decided to offer a course in Hotel and Tourism it realized that a significant group of potential students were those already working within the industry but who could not simply take time off work to attend the campus. It also identified many who were in senior positions within the industry and who would prefer not to study alongside relatively 'junior' staff within their hotel! The logical decision was to offer the course in a self-instructional format.

Conventional course structures

It is very easy for us to fall into the trap of mounting the course that we feel learners need and in a form that they will want. However, are the topics the ones that learners want to study? Are the administration and conduct of the course the most effective and efficient for them?

The National Association of Clinical Tutors ran a programme of seminars for those senior medical staff, Clinical Tutors, who trained junior doctors in hospitals. Unfortunately these Clinical Tutors often spent more time travelling to the venue to attend the programme than taking part in it! Furthermore, the different backgrounds and experiences of the tutors meant that not all tutors benefited equally from the programme that was offered.

A survey of Clinical Tutors revealed not only the topics that they felt were most important, including their depth and scope, but that a self-instructional format would be appropriate for much of it. The resulting printed package (NACT, 1992) focused on the topics the tutors had identified, included core and optional material, and was entirely self-instructional. The time they engaged in study was less than the time they had previously spent driving to the seminars!

The MSC definition also includes the phrase about enabling people to learn 'at a time, place and pace that suits them best'; the slogan used by the Open Tech in the late 1980s. Evidence from the Open University reveals, contrary to original beliefs, that students do not study at the same times and days during the week. Typically learners fit their study around their lives – studying at times convenient to themselves. Similarly, not all students have the luxury of a study – many use the kitchen table once the cooking and clearing up has been done, or retreat to the bedroom. With regard to pace, it depends upon the background, previous experience and interests of the learner. Not all students study the material in the same depth. Some admit to getting 'side-tracked' because the topic or whatever was particularly interesting, while others skip over the same material. Perhaps the best example of a student studying at a time, place and pace that suited him was the bus driver mentioned earlier. He had his study material in his cab and at the start and end of his route spent 10 minutes studying. Sometimes he would complete whole pages in 10 minutes, but at other times he would need to reread a section several times. He fitted most of his study into 10 minutes - and did so over a number of years!

You may think that the definition by Webberley and Haffenden is virtually the same as that from the MSC. It talks about studying at home or work and at a convenient pace. Perhaps you feel the phrase in the MSC definition about 'arrangements to enable people to learn' is the same as the points in the Webberley and Haffenden definition about enrolling at any time, gaining access to the things they need and completing the course when they want to. Indeed, I suspect that if you were asked to identify an institution that illustrated the commitment to open learning, assuming you are in the UK, you might identify the Open University.

Unfortunately, although you may be able to enrol at any time, the courses only commence at one date in the year. If you apply too late you may have to wait another year! It may be that you already have various skills and experience and really have no need for the teaching the course provides – all that you want is the qualification.

Unfortunately, many Open University courses require a series of assignments to be completed at specific times during the year and an examination to be taken on one particular day. Furthermore, depending on the actual course, tutorial support is provided whether you want it or not. Fortunately, other institutions are more flexible.

The Hotel and Institutional Catering Management Association, like many other commercial and industrial organizations, operates a policy for the Accreditation of Prior Learning (APL). If applicants have acquired the skills and techniques specified, no matter where they acquired them and over what period, they are given recognition without having to go through a course they do not need. The Open Learning Agency of Australia allows students to register at three different times in the year. To be fair, the Open University course P521 *Developing an Open Learning Package* offers tutorial support and guidance at an additional cost.

The definition provided by Phil Race includes several of the key elements already identified, but phrases these somewhat differently. He also says clearly that open learning should 'open up various choices and degrees of control to learners'. The comments about the Open University, above, indicate that it really isn't very open – but how open is your institution? How much choice would you like to give students? Over 10 years ago Roger Lewis (1986, page 8) argued that:

> In a completely open system, learners can learn whatever they wish, for whatever reasons, wherever they choose, however they choose. But schemes are never totally open in these ways.

He provided a list of questions which help to determine the degree of choice a student has (Lewis, 1986, page 6):

Why they learn	The extent to which the motivation is their own
What they learn	The extent to which they construct their own context
How they learn	The extent to which they choose the methods and route to suit their own ways of learning
Where they learn	The extent to which they choose the learning environment
When they learn	The extent to which they choose when to start, their pace and when to finish
How their learning	The extent to which they decide *when* a subject will be measured: their learning to assessed, *what sort* of assessment and *who* will help them carry it out
Who can help them	The extent to which they decide who is best placed to help and when
What they do next	The extent to which they decide what they want to do next (eg further courses, jobs)

In terms of openness Lewis provided a table which incorporated these and other questions to illustrate a continuum between open and closed institutions. The beauty of the table is that you can use it to assess how open, or closed, your institution is. I reproduce the table as Figure 3.3. You may decide to share it with your colleagues in assessing the openness of your institution or ways in which you could make it more open.

Basic Question	Closed ←	Aspects	→ Open
Who?	Scheme open to select groups only		Scheme open to all
	Set entry requirements, eg traditional exam success		Self-assessment and diagnostic facilities
	Scheme not marketed		Extensive publicity, regularly updated information
Why?	Choice made by others, eg tutor, employer		Learner choice
	No counselling or guidance		Pre-entry counselling
What?	Entire syllabus set out in advance, eg by validating body; no choice possible within it		Learner formulates own objectives and syllabus
	Limited to materials the tutor has produced		Uses wide range of materials drawn from many sources
	Whole course must be taken		Content tailored to need; individual learners can take different modules
	No guidance on selection of content		Guidance on selection of content
	Knowledge, facts, 'academic'		Experience, practice, feeling, attitude
	No recognition of past experience		Credits given for past experience
How?	Only one method/style provided for; little variation in learner activity		Choice of learning methods/styles; varied activities
	One route only through material		Choice of routes through material
	Package in one medium only		Package uses variety of media
Where?	One place only (eg at work)		Learner chooses place (eg home, work, while travelling)
	Regular fixed attendance required		Learner can attend, or not – as desired
	Practical work requires fixed attendance		Practical work offered through kits and/or drop-in access and/or place of work itself
When?	Fixed starting date(s)		Start any time
	Learner placed by a fixed timetable		Learner decides pace of work
	Fixed ending		End at any time
How is the learner doing?	Externally mixed method of assessment eg formal exam		Variety of assessment methods; learner choice of assessment methods; learner constructs method of assessment
	Normative assessment		Criteria/competency-based assessment
	No feedback on performance		Frequent, full, on-going feedback on performance, available as desired
	Assessment dates fixed and non-negotiable		Learner decides when to be assessed
	Assessment available only for whole course		Assessment available for each module
Who can help the learner?	No support outside course/package		Variety of possible kinds of support (eg advice, guidance, counselling)
	Only professional supporters (eg teachers) encouraged		Non-professional, as well as professional supporters; informal as well as formal support encouraged (eg mentor, family friends)
	Support available only in one place, eg training centre		Support available in many places
	Support available in one mode only, eg face-to-face		Support available in a variety of modes, eg letter, telephone, face-to-face
What does it lead to?	One destination		Various possible destinations

(This table first appeared in 'What is open learning?' and is reprinted with the permission of the Council for Educational Technology.)

Notes
1. It is possible to increase or to reduce the number of basic questions used to analyse a scheme.
2. It is also possible to increase or to reduce the number of aspects of each question. You can see, for example, that I have given two aspects for *why?* and six for *what?*
3. All schemes will in practice be open on some aspects and closed on others, either through choice or through lack of resources.
4. Some parts of a scheme, eg different modules or practical work, may be open to a different extent, or in different ways, from other parts of the same scheme.

Figure 3.3 *The open–closed learning continuum*

The definitions of open learning identify several of the key elements involved in overcoming barriers, providing access and learner control. In reviewing this definition and others it is fairly easy to spot these key elements – it is more difficult to spot those that may be missing. What elements do you think may be missing from these definitions?

A major concern for most learners, in addition to the prerequisites and study time, resultant qualification and so on, is how much money it will cost. Is the course open to those who can afford it? The cost may not merely be the registration fee. If we simply ignore buying paper and pens, stamps and travel costs (which may not be insignificant for many), learners may also have to buy books and equipment and attend face-to-face or residential sessions. While learners are doing this, assuming they are adults, they may have to give up earning overtime payments, employ child minders or give up holidays. Following an open learning course can be expensive and a course may exclude as many people as it attracts.

3.3 Distance learning and flexible learning

I have spent some time discussing the definitions of open learning and associated key elements because these are central to any subsequent consideration of distance and flexible learning. It is also because I suspect that you and your colleagues would have plenty to say about open learning but progressively less and less to say about distance and flexible learning respectively. In fact, if you were expecting a similar discussion of distance learning and flexible learning to that which I provided on open learning you are going to be disappointed; let me explain why.

To determine a working definition of distance learning you could, of course, compare your colleagues' personal definitions with existing ones and reach a group consensus; you could repeat Alternatives A and B outlined above. In Figure 3.4 I have assembled several definitions of distance learning that would enable you to do this. (You could always supplement these definitions with others of your choice.)

If you were to do this I suspect that very soon you would come to the conclusion that the key feature of the definitions, not surprisingly, was that of geographical location – learners are physically distant from teachers or trainers; they are separated by time and space. In terms of the question we started with on page 24 the main distinction is that open learning refers to *principles* of access to learning, learner choice and control, while distance learning merely refers to the *method of learning*. Open learning involves distance learning as a method of instruction but not all distance learning is open; it may not satisfy the main principles.

The reason why I suspect that you and your colleagues would have little to say about flexible learning is that it is extremely difficult to locate definitions that are of a similar form to those for open learning. In her book on *Key Terms and Issues in Open and Distance Learning*, Barbara Hodgson (1993, page 53) explained:

Distance learning is learning while at a distance from one's teacher – usually with the help of pre-recorded, packaged learning materials. The learners are separated from their teachers in time and space but are still guided by them.

Rowntree (1992, page 29)

All learners who use self-instructional materials whether in open, distance or flexible systems are, to some extent, distance learners. The use of self-instructional materials implies that learners are studying at one remove from the author who, by preparing the learning materials, is effectively their principal teacher. Even in those systems where face-to-face tutorial support is provided there is rarely any guarantee that the support tutor is permanently available. Indeed, the fact that learners can pursue their studies in their own way, in their own time and in places of their choosing is probably the biggest single advantage of, and motive for, providing self-instructional materials. All learners who use materials of this kind, then, are either actual or potential distance learners.

Hodgson (1993, pages 41–2)

- the quasi-permanent separation of teacher and learner throughout the length of the learning process (this distinguishes it from conventional face-to-face education)
- the influence of an educational organization both in the planning and preparation of learning materials and in the provision of student support services (this distinguishes it from private study and teach-yourself programmes)
- the use of technical media – print, audio, video or computer – to unite teacher and learner and carry the content of the course
- the provision of two-way communication so that the student may benefit from or even initiate dialogue (this distinguishes it from other uses of technology in education)
- the quasi-permanent absence of the learning group throughout the length of the learning process so that people are usually taught as individuals rather than in groups, with the possibility of occasional meetings, either face-to-face or by electronic means, for both didactic and socialization purposes.

Keegan (1996, page 50)

Figure 3.4 *Definitions of distance learning*

Flexible learning is a term used to describe many learning systems which could just as well be called 'open'. The word 'flexible' tends to emphasize the individual nature of the programme; that it is designed to offer the maximum opportunity to every possible learner. A definition offered by the National Council for Educational Technology is:

> ...a means of making it possible for learners to gain access to education and training provision tailored to their needs and aspirations.

The term is sometimes favoured because people believe it makes more obvious what is implied than does 'open learning'. Flexible learning is no more tightly defined than is open learning and the terms are often used synonymously.

A similar focus was offered by the TVEI Flexible Learning Development programme. The system of flexible learning was designed to... meet the learning needs of students as individuals and in groups... and to give the student increasing responsibility for his/her own learning within a framework of support.

If you and your colleagues considered your personal definitions of flexible learning I suspect that it would suggest that the key feature you identified was that of *delivery* – whether in an open or distance learning context. However, if some of your colleagues were not unduly concerned about the terminology, or had different preferences, they would be in good company. Derek Rowntree (1992, page 1) talks about:

> ...a family of approaches to education and training that mostly call themselves "open learning" or "distance learning". But there are many offspring and sundry relatives going by a profusion of other names – flexible learning, supported self-study, technology-based training, and so on.

In a later book, *Preparing Materials for Open, Distance and Flexible Learning*, he remarks (Rowntree, 1994, page 2):

> Open learning? Distance learning? Flexible learning? Which are you concerned with? Maybe some combination of the three. Or perhaps your form of learning goes under another name. No matter.

Elsewhere, in *The Open Learning Handbook*, Phil Race considers the three terms – open, distance and flexible learning – and comes to the conclusion that (Race, 1994, pages 22–3):

> 'flexible learning' is the most satisfactory of the three terms. Both 'open learning' in its broadest sense, and 'distance learning' as a sub-set of open learning, involve giving learners some degree of choice and control. In other words, they introduce elements of flexibility into the learning process... 'open learning' is the one that's best known, and I've chosen to use it in most parts of this book, even though I'd often prefer to use the word 'flexible'!

If these people are not unduly concerned you have no need to be. Perhaps it is sufficient to equate open learning with *principles*, distance learning with *methods* and flexible learning with *delivery*.

References

Hodgson, B (1993) *Key Terms and Issues in Open and Distance Learning*, Kogan Page, London.

Keegan, D (1996) *Foundations of Distance Education*, Routledge, London.

Lewis, R (1986) What is open learning? *Open Learning*, 1(1), 5–10.

Lockwood, F G and Lewis, K (1994) Future growth areas in the use of self-instructional materials: optimum investment in personnel and exploitation of their expertise. A paper presented at the ICDE Pacific Rim Conference, Wellington, New Zealand, 8–12 May.

Manpower Services Commission (1984) *A New Training Initiative*, Manpower Services Commission, Sheffield.

NACT (1992) *NACT Training Package*, National Association of Clinical Tutors, 6 St Andrews Place, London NW1 4LB.

Race, P (1994) *The Open Learning Handbook*, Kogan Page, London.

Rowntree, D (1992) *Exploring Open and Distance Learning*, Kogan Page, London.

Rowntree, D (1994) *Preparing Materials for Open, Distance and Flexible Learning*, Kogan Page, London.

Webberley, R and Haffenden, I (1987) Skills training and responsive management. In *Open Learning for Adults* (eds M. Thorpe and D. Grugeon), Longman, Harlow.

Chapter 4

Resources and constraints

A review of the resources available and the constraints within which you must work is an essential preliminary to planning any package of self-instructional materials or setting up an open or flexible learning system. Your intention should be to ensure that significant aspects that may either contribute to the task, or detract from it, are not overlooked. A typical failing is to underestimate the influence of likely constraints.

Depending upon your perspective, some aspects associated with material/system planning may be regarded as either resources or constraints – the task is for you to decide their significance. The following questions are designed to help you consider a number of these aspects.

1. **What funds are available for course planning, production and presentation/setting up the system?**
   (Consider not only the cost of materials – drafts and final form, but also cost of personnel – initial and recurrent costs and the costs of introducing the new system.)

2. **What level of commitment or contribution is available from colleagues?**
   (Consider the contributions of institutional staff in writing/assembling materials and commenting. Support staff in drafting and administration and their other commitments.)

3. **What is the time-scale within which materials will be produced/the new system introduced?**
   (Consider what planning and production schedule may be needed and the implications this may have for the materials/introducing the new system.)

4. **What published materials are available and what implications could these have for inclusion in the course?**

   (Consider what texts, tapes, photos, maps, charts, etc., could be used, including their availability and how appropriate they are.)

5. **What additional equipment and backup may be necessary?**

   (Consider the use of materials in open and distance learning contexts, including the arrangements that may be necessary for learners to study in libraries, at workstations or at home.)

4.1 What funds are available for course planning, production and presentation/setting up the system?

You may know exactly the funds you have available and the budget you have to work within, or you may not. Whatever the position, it is vital that you consider those 'things' – be they people, services or materials – that are going to cost money and consider the budget or the implications of what you are planning carefully before you embark on it. We all know that it is possible to hide costs – we may not be billed for official photocopying or postage, we do unofficial favours for people or work outside our timetable or job description – but somewhere a cost is involved.

Given the pointer of those 'things' that are likely to cost money (people, services and materials), it is likely that a small group brainstorm will come up with a whole range of items; some of these are presented in Figure 4.1. You can add to or amend this list to suit your particular purposes.

4.1.1 Releasing institutional staff from existing duties

People are likely to be the most expensive item in any project involving the production or assembly of self-instructional materials or the system which operates it. If academic, technical or managerial staff are to be involved they will need to be released from other commitments. This may mean that some tasks are simply not done or that other people are brought in to do them. When thinking about the cost of people it is easy to think only of whole/part posts or specific periods when trying to estimate such staff costs. However, other costs can be significant.

A short while ago I heard of an Australian colleague who had devised a small portable digital display unit into which he could punch the estimated salaries of those in the room (those taking part in the meeting). The device then computed and displayed the cost to the institution of every minute the meeting lasted. It can be a sobering thought to consider that the time (the cost) taken to decide on an item was more than it cost!

- releasing institutional staff from existing duties
- employing other individuals as consultants, academic/technical assessors, external examiners, tutors and mentors
- employing secretarial and support staff to assist with materials production
- developing prototype materials (kits, models, project work and apparatus)
- producing printed, audio, video and computer-based materials
- packing, handling, storing and mailing/delivery
- revision and remake/update of materials
- clerical and administrative staff and systems to aid course production and presentation

Figure 4.1 *Cost of materials production and presentation*

4.1.2 Employing other individuals as consultants, academic assessors, external examiners, tutors and mentors

Depending on the budget, the nature of the materials/system being produced or your needs, you may decide to employ individuals outside your institution. A consultant may enable you to avoid pitfalls and problems that would consume time, effort and money. An academic assessor may challenge or support the academic or technical content of the materials – giving reassurance or by raising an issue at an early stage avoiding major problems at a future date. You may even accept that you do not have the academic/technical knowledge or skill in a particular area and appoint someone to assemble or write the required material. An external examiner may give advice and credibility to the project that is cheap compared with the modest fees or honorarium given. Part-time tutors, teaching assistants and workplace mentors can provide learner support – but at a cost.

Of course, in each of these cases you will need to seek other advice as to the most appropriate level of fee. However, in my experience people often make contributions to such projects from a genuine interest and not the level of fee involved; they would often earn more 'washing dishes' than completing the task in hand at the hourly rate paid.

4.1.3 Employing secretarial and support staff to assist with material production

It can be a serious mistake to overlook the contribution that secretarial and support staff make towards materials production and presentation. Of course, if you are happy to become the highest paid photocopying operator, two-fingered typist, telephonist, collator of papers, filler of envelopes and licker of stamps, continue to overlook it.

It is also a serious mistake to believe that existing secretarial and support staff can simply take on additional tasks and responsibilities; that they have both the skills and time required. A consideration of the tasks they will need to perform is the basis of a job specification to identify, train or recruit the support you will need.

4.1.4 Developing prototype materials (Kits, models, project work, apparatus)

If your self-instructional material involves Home Experiment Kits (HEKs), models or apparatus, you not only have to cost the time and effort of locating or developing these, but also that of assembling multiple copies of them (assuming your learners need a copy each).

The kit or materials may be modest or elaborate. The Open University assembled extremely elaborate kits for students studying the science foundation course. It contained the chemicals, equipment and apparatus they would need to perform a whole range of experiments and essentially brought the science laboratory into the homes of students. In contrast, an early version of the Open University Science Preparatory materials provided students with a packet of watercress seeds and instructions on how to conduct an elaborate experiment involving their germination and growth under a variety of conditions. Students supplied their own sauces and toilet paper on which to grow the seedlings, and they provided their own drinking glasses, cups and translucent disposable plastic cup to cover the seeds/seedlings and to create different growing environments. While the kit itself may be extremely modest – a packet of seeds – the cost of devising the associated experiments may be substantial.

When the Society of Cosmetic Scientists were assembling their Distance Learning Course (Society of Cosmetic Scientists, 1995) one task they faced was the teaching of perfumery at a distance. They had to select the liquids to smell and the smelling strips to use, and had to produce a printed study guide to give directions and an audio tape to provide instructions (thus leaving eyes, hands and nose free); these were some of the obvious costs of assembling the prototype. Less obvious, but equally important were the costs of selecting leak-proof bottles, ensuring that safety regulations (COOSH regulations) were satisfied during their use and eventual disposal, that all vials were labelled in accordance with EC legislation, that outer packaging was appropriate and surcharges paid to those delivering packages containing chemicals, and so on and so on.

Sometimes it may be far more cost-effective to purchase multiple copies, or permission to copy, than trying to assemble things from scratch. Some detective work to find a supplier of plastic molecular models – to enable students to make molecular structures from the basic elements – may be far more cost-effective than trying to make the models yourself. Purchasing sheet music may be more cost-effective than allowing colleagues to spend hours composing.

4.1.5 Producing printed, audio, video and computer-based materials

Print is cheap, versatile and portable. It is likely that a considerable part of your teaching material will be in print. As such, it is worth considering precisely how much it will cost to produce, say, a 48 page A4 booklet. As soon as you start to do this you will be asked a whole series of questions – about paper quality, type of binding, use of colour – both in the body of the text and as a cover. You will also be asked how many copies you need. The size of print run is likely to dictate the reproduction technique you chose – printing or photocopying. A recent technical development has been the growth in 'on-demand printing', such as the DocuTech system offered by Rank Xerox. In these systems it is possible to provide either an online or disk copy of the original and for the required number of copies to be produced, backed up, collated and bounded by high-speed photocopying; a few minutes per finished booklet at less than £2 per 48 page booklet is typical.

In contrast, audio and video materials are substantially more expensive. It would obviously depend upon the form of production and any materials involved, but a typical cost for audio-visual materials, such as a combination of audiotape linked to visuals – diagrams, photographs, maps, charts, etc. – would be £100 per minute. For video material, studio and simple one- or two-camera work is obviously cheaper than outside filming using guest speakers and archive or copyright material. However, as a guideline you could expect to pay close to £1000 per minute for video material. This, of course, is merely the cost of the original. If you want multiple copies you will not only have the cost of blank cassettes but also duplication costs.

4.1.6 Packing, handling, storing and mailing/delivery

You will also have the cost of packing, handling and storing – be it print, audio/video materials or other components. When the Society of Cosmetic Scientists (SCS) were assembling a mini Home Experiment Kit (HEK) they first considered using an expanded polystyrene block, about 22 cm × 32 cm × 5.5 cm, with spaces formed into it to hold the various chemicals, pieces of apparatus, etc. The HEK was to be non-returnable. Indeed, in the past organizations have learned, to their embarrassment, that the cost of returning an item, checking and storing it is more expensive than merely supplying it! Enquiries revealed that the cost of the disposable, polystyrene slab, to the desired specification, was about £6 each! The high cost was mainly due to the costs of making the die from which subsequent blocks would be moulded. The alternative, to use a cardboard box, complete with slots and support, was not only more environmentally friendly, but less than half the cost.

4.1.7 Revision and remake/update of materials

Next time you watch a soccer match or live theatrical performance, just think about the reserve player on the bench or the understudy in the wings. Each of these situations, and many others, holds someone in reserve in case they are needed. Everyone knows that it is expensive to have this talent merely sitting around, but if 'the show is to go on' it is an expense they have to accept.

You will obviously be trying to assemble the most effective and efficient teaching package possible. However, I would suggest that it would be a mistake to commit all your funds and all your resources for the production to the material with no consideration of revision or update. Just as it is prudent to commit a small proportion of your funds to conduct your consumer survey or Training Needs Analysis to ensure that you have a market for your product or audience for your course, it is prudent to keep a small proportion of your resources in reserve for changes, revisions and refinements.

There is certainly no point monitoring a course and collecting feedback and learner opinions, etc. if you have no resources to do anything about the problems you discover! You may need to build time into people's work-plans or contracts so that they are available, if necessary, to revise their previous material. You may be able to contract an individual who didn't write the previous material to make changes to it in light of evaluations. The SCS was able to use both of these strategies. On the basis of feedback the original authors were invited to revise/update their teaching materials for subsequent presentation. Other subject matter experts were employed to revise former texts according to the detailed brief given. However, in each case fees were involved for both authors and editors.

4.1.8 Clerical and administrative staff to aid course production

The scale of your project will obviously dictate the need, or otherwise, for additional clerical/administrative staff. The danger, of course, is in assuming that a modest project involving, say, 30–40 learners, also involves a modest amount of clerical/administrative support. The existing staff may be more than prepared to process additional application forms, receive incoming assignments, collate grades, return scripts, etc.

However, who will be responsible for liaising with the printer over copies of the course materials, ensuring that tapes are copied and packages mailed or delivered to students, and that queries from students are answered or redirected to colleagues? Where does the division of responsibility lay? What if students want an extension on an assignment? Who will arrange access for a factory, school or office visit?

The SCS previously relied upon a London College to administer the conventionally taught course. However, the creation of a distance learning course for about 75 students per year necessitated the employment of a part-time course administrator. Her task was to respond to all enquirers, register students and maintain a detailed database of them. Although all financial aspects were forwarded to an accountant, the administrator did receive any academic and technical queries associated with the course and forwarded these to the appropriate author.

4.2 What level of commitment or contribution is available from colleagues?

It is usual that when some new initiative or project is announced there is a flurry of interest. Unfortunately, expressions of 'interest' are simply not enough if all the tasks associated with producing quality teaching material are to be accomplished in the time available. Who is going to provide what, over what period and when are critical questions in any planning activity. A practical way of determining the commitment or contribution from colleagues is to assemble a course proposal which specifies each individual's contribution – the precise nature of the contribution and when it will be made. In Figure 4.2 I have divided potential contributors into three groups: academic or technical staff, support staff and others.

Academic or technical staff   – plan content, course structure, order and sequence

– undertake reading and research

– draft and redraft material; comment on drafts

– tutor the course, mark scripts and examinations

– steer proposal through committees

– liaise with outside agencies

Support staff   – assemble drafts and final copy of artwork, photographs, charts, etc

– liaise with printers, packers, distributors

Others   – external consultants, academic assessors, media producers

– internal advisers/specialists

Figure 4.2 *Level of commitment*

4.2.1 Academic staff

How much time will teachers and trainers have to plan the course content, its structure and sequence, and over what period? They may have the academic or technical content at their fingertips, or they may need to undertake reading and research to obtain the information they are going to teach. How much time will academic staff have to draft and redraft material, comment on the materials of others and steer course proposals through committees? It may be necessary to liaise with outside agencies, such as other teaching, training or employers' organizations. Who will have responsibility for these tasks? Will staff be involved in tutoring the course, providing personal or counselling support to learners? Will they be involved in marking assignments and examinations, and if so how much time will be allocated for these tasks?

4.2.2 Support staff

Secretaries and clerical and support staff have job specifications. Is it possible to specify who will be responsible for typing drafts and when the manuscripts will be available? Who will be responsible for liaising with printers, packers and the deliverers of the teaching material? If material is to be provided as Web pages or on a CD-ROM, who will transform, text, audio and video files into an appropriate form? Will someone have the job of monitoring the whole course production exercise?

4.2.3 Others

If photographs, maps, charts and other artwork are to be assembled, who will brief the producers? Under what terms (contract or agreement) will photographs be taken, maps drawn and artwork produced?

It may be that external consultants will be asked to assemble parts of the teaching material. If so, it is likely that academic and/or clerical staff will be involved in briefing or monitoring its production. It is not unusual for external academic or technical assessors to be appointed.

For each of these tasks it is necessary to be clear who will be responsible, how much time they have available and when. In my experience by far the best way is to draw up a proposal or contract that makes it completely clear. If the people involved are employees of the organization the agreement will indicate how this is part of their job – it is what they are paid for! If they are employed as consultants, the agreement will make clear the nature of the contract.

4.3 What is the time-scale within which materials will be produced and the new system introduced?

For our purposes the time-scale is simply the period between the conception of the course or project and its eventual study by learners. For most organizations and groups it is considered in weeks and months rather than years (see Chapter 6). In considering the main elements you may find it useful to divide the exercise into three stages (negotiation with gatekeepers, overall plan, detailed schedule) and then think how these are related.

4.3.1 Negotiation with gatekeepers

It isn't sufficient to identify a teaching or training need, devise a method of satisfying it and then produce the material. If you need funds, academic or departmental approval and the cooperation of others there will undoubtedly be key committees, boards or individuals to convince; these are the gatekeepers for approval. A list follows of the various Open University committees and boards that would need to be approached if a proposed course was to be given approval.

- Faculty Board
- Academic Board
- Residential Schools Committee
- Tuition and Counselling Committee
- Broadcast and Audio Visual Sub-Committee
- Course Development Committee
- Examinations and Assessment Committee

Although these are the key committees and boards, within each it is likely that sub-groups would consider proposals and comment on them. For example, within the Faculty Board a Curriculum Sub-Group may comment on the implications of the proposed course within the overall profile of courses on offer by the faculty. A Manpower Planning Sub-Group may comment on the availability of academic personnel if the proposed course is approved and so on. There would undoubtedly be key individuals to approach, such as the secretaries of committees to ensure that proposals are in an appropriate form, the Head of Reprographics to ensure there is sufficient capacity to produce printed materials, and the Head of Information Technology to ensure that the system can cope with another *online* course.

Jan Feb Mar Apr May Jun Jul Aug Sep Oct Nov Dec

Year 1

Year 2

Jan Feb Mar Apr May Jun Jul Aug Sep Oct Nov Dec

Committees and Boards	Date(s) of meetings
1.	
2.	
3.	
4.	
5.	

Other gatekeepers

1.	2.
3.	4.

Figure 4.3 *Course planning: negotiation with gatekeepers*

The list is not unduly long. In many large organizations committees and boards do not meet on request but to a committee timetable. Unless you can secure 'chairman's action' for your request, which may be unlikely, you will have to wait until the next meeting! If your envisaged schedule is in terms of weeks or months this delay could be significant – the difference between success and failure. As a result you may feel that it would be a sobering exercise to consider which committees, boards, etc. you and your colleagues would need to contact if a course is to be given approval; this is assuming it clears each hurdle first time!

In Figure 4.3 I simply offer a 24 month grid which should span your time-scale. For the purpose of the exercise you could:

1. Agree that the date of the exercise marks the starting point of the time-scale and mark this on the grid.
2. Agree the date when the envisaged course will be available for study and mark this on the grid.
3. Identify the key committees and boards that would need to provide approval and the dates they meet, and mark these on the grid.
4. Identify other key gatekeepers who would need to be approached and whose support would be needed.

You may have a fully worked up proposal and committees and boards that meet on request. You may yet have to assemble the proposal and begin the process of gaining support. The exercise may reveal that the identification and negotiation with gatekeepers may take longer than you think.

4.3.2 Overall plan

It is likely that you will need an overall plan as part of your negotiation with gatekeepers – a plan that is realistic. In devising your plan you will need to identify the main parts: the procedures you intend to incorporate and how they fit into your timetable. Unfortunately there is no model timetable. It is typically a question of how much time have you got – not how much time do you want! However, I can offer an example (Figure 4.4) that illustrates some of the points you will need to consider. It is a simplified version of the actual schedule that was adopted for the developmental testing of the Open University course EH221 *Educational Computing* (a procedure whereby the course was piloted before it was finalized and offered to students).

Computer programmes are readily available that will assemble production timetables from the information you provide. The typical Gantt chart can be an invaluable aid in monitoring course production (Freeman, 1997)

The preliminary negotiations had been completed with gatekeepers and the necessary approvals granted. The first meeting of the whole team was at the end of May. Contributors, working in four small groups, would have four and a half months to assembled first drafts (D1s) of the four main parts of the course – Blocks A to D; each block equivalent to about 50 hours of study time (see Figure 4.4) A whole team meeting was held in mid-October to approve the material in Block A

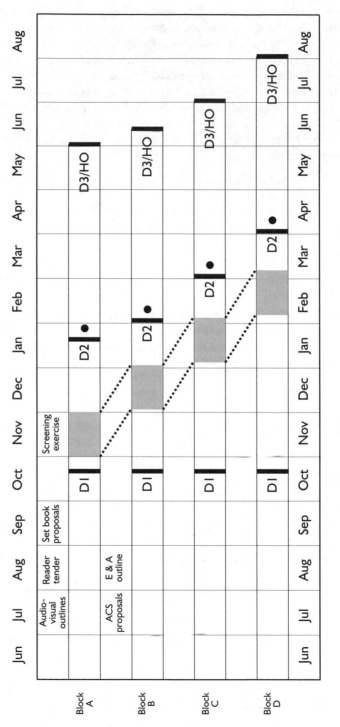

Figure 4.4 *Simplified production schedule*

that would be studied by a representative group of students in a screening exercise planned for November. At the end of this screening exercise the information collected would be presented to the authors, who would have about six weeks to assemble the second draft (D2) which would be discussed by the whole team in late January. As a result of this meeting, and consideration of the other elements making up the Block, authors would have approximately four months to assemble the third or handover draft (D3/HO). A final whole-team meeting would approve Block A for handover and actual duplication. A similar schedule was adopted for Blocks B, C and D. You will note that the timing of the screening exercise was staggered so that the same group of students could study each of the four blocks in turn – in exactly the same way that real students would.

In assembling your overall plan you will need to decide:

- how much time you have between initial course conception and the date of handover
- the number of drafts you intend to produce between synopsis and final version
- what form of screening, piloting or testing of the materials you intend before you agree the final version.

You will also need to assure yourself that those responsible for reproducing texts, tapes and kits can do all of this between D3/HO and the date it must be available for study by students.

4.3.3 Detailed schedule

Overall plans are vital – but so is a detailed schedule that unpacks the overall plan. For example, if the whole team is to be able to offer advice and assistance on the material in the 50 hour Block A it would take time to circulate the draft and colleagues would need some time to consider it prior to the meeting. How much time would you allocate for circulation and study of the material? Depending on your estimates, the authors would probably have less than four months to assemble their D1 – especially if it was to be assembled in a form that could be readily revised for study in the Screening Exercise.

Figure 4.5 represents part of the detailed schedule that was assembled for the production of some self-instruction material within a hospitality and catering course.

You will see that two weeks were allowed for an author to assemble a synopsis (D0) of the content, there was a meeting in the following week and a further two weeks to assemble the first draft (D1) before a second meeting and so on. A first glance may suggest a tight but realistic schedule. Two weeks to assemble a 500 word synopsis doesn't sound unrealistic – especially if the author is a specialist and has the information at his or her fingertips. However, it isn't really two weeks but more like one week if time is to be allowed for circulating the typescript and allowing people a day or so to read it. Similarly, authors do not have two weeks to revise the D1 into a D2 if time is to be allowed for typing up the manuscript, circulating it and giving time for study. Two weeks in August may seem reasonable, just like two weeks to prepare the trial version may seem reasonable. However, early August is the peak holiday season in the UK – will people be available and willing to work on the material? An overall plan is useful, but needs a detailed schedule to confirm that it is realistic.

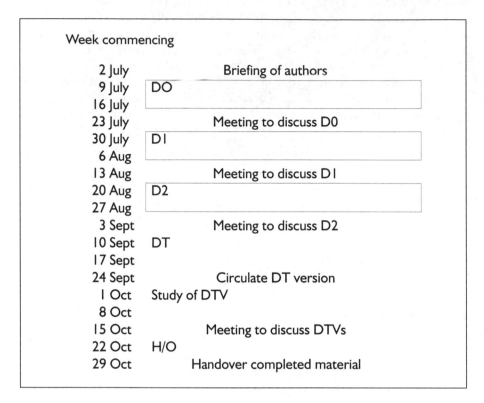

Figure 4.5 *Detailed production schedule*

Following on from your exercise to identify the gatekeepers within your organization, you may find it useful to provide further two-year grids and consider how much time is needed between starting the project and having it available for study.

4.4 What published materials are available and what implications could these have for inclusion in the course?

There is no shortage of published materials that are available to you; the libraries are full of them (see Figure 4.6). A survey of databases like the one provided by the International Centre for Distance Learning (http://www-icdl.open.ac.uk) may identify existing multimedia courses that are already in existence and save you the trouble of creating one. Other reviews of databases like that of the British Association for Open Learning may identify self-instructional books and other textbooks and training manuals. Other sources, such as the National Open Learning Library, may identify articles in journals, magazines and newspapers (see also Rowntree, 1992). You and your colleagues will undoubtedly have teaching notes, case study materials, worksheets, simulations and role plays – a whole host of resources to draw upon. You may even have already identified TV broadcasts and radio programmes as well as instructional video programmes that could be part of your teaching. There may be computer-based materials, apparatus and kits that could be modified for your use.

- Structured multimedia courses or teaching material
- Self-instructional books
- Textbooks
- Handbooks, training manuals
- Articles in journals, magazines, newspapers
- Resource packs, leaflets, publicity material
- Lecture notes, case studies
- Worksheets, exercises, simulations, role plays
- Broadcast TV and radio programmes
- Instructional video programmes
- Computer-based training materials
- Kits and equipment

Figure 4.6 *Published material available*

The arguments for using existing materials are strong. Some of these are summarized in Figure 4.7 under the headings Cost, Time, Breadth, Quality, Skills and Stress.

4.4.1 Cost

It is expensive to develop new teaching materials, with the major cost being people's salaries; the cost of print and other media is likely to be small in comparison with the expenditure on human resources. While they are devising new teaching materials they are not doing other things. Costs associated with secretarial and clerical costs, printing, handling, storing, record-keeping and monitoring can consume scarce resources.

4.4.2 Time

It takes both time and effort to write new material – possibly more than you think. It also takes time to type up, correct, copy, circulate, revise, test and so on. All of these need to fit realistically into a time plan – taking due account of personal and national holidays, festivals, etc.

Cost	– Expensive to develop new materials
	– Consume scarce institutional resources
Time	– Time and effort to write new material
Breadth	– Exposure to different sources, viewpoints, treatments
Quality	– Unable to improve on existing material in the time and with the resources available
Skills	– Lack of appropriate skills
	– Training may or may not be available
Stress	– Avoid stress and pressure involved in materials design and production

Figure 4.7 *Why use existing material?*

4.4.3 Breadth

Drawing upon existing materials may give your learners exposure to different sources, different viewpoints and different treatments. Indeed, students may be encouraged to compare and contrast these differences.

4.4.4 Quality

If you are honest you may be unable to improve upon the quality of the existing materials in the time available and with the resources at your disposal.

4.4.5 Skills

Assembling self-instructional materials, be they printed, computer-based or using new communications media, requires a high degree of skill. Staff may not have the appropriate skills. The training may or may not be available on the time-scale within which you are working.

4.4.6 Stress

Many of those who have been involved in the production of a self-instructional package have likened it to a treadmill that, once started, doesn't stop until the job is done. Your previous consideration of the outline plan and detailed schedule indicates the problems caused by the failure of any one individual to deliver the materials on time. Many have breathed a sign of relief when the final materials were handed over, saying, 'Done it. No one was sick, no one resigned, no one died, no one took their holidays'.

Using existing materials can avoid the stress and pressure involved in designing and producing self-instructional materials.

If the arguments for using existing materials are so strong, why would anyone not use them? Some possible reasons are listed in Figure 4.8.

- No existing materials suitable
- Target audience has particular needs
- Difficult to adapt existing material
- Belief that 'I can do better' – 'not invented here'
- Underestimate the task (cost, time, skill, difficulty)
- Academic staff want to try writing
- Academic staff desire recognition by peers

Figure 4.8 *Why people do not use existing materials*

After reviewing all the databases available, colleagues have come to the conclusion that there really is nothing suitable. They often argue that the audience that has been identified has unique needs – needs that no other course is able to satisfy. When asked about the possibility of adapting existing material, it is not unusual for colleagues to argue that in the time it would take to modify existing material they could write it themselves! There is often the belief that 'I can do better', it should be generated *in house* – indicators of the 'not invented here' mentality.

A common feature is for colleagues to underestimate what is involved in the task (Figure 4.8) – the time it is likely to consume and the skills needed. They may want a change from previous conventional teaching and see this as a logical, painless progression. A driving force is often the realization that in producing self-instructional material the institution will be going public, that the teaching or training materials that were normally private and restricted documents shared between teacher and learner are now to become public documents. In such circumstances it is not unusual for colleagues to want the recognition that goes with authorship – having their name on the front cover.

4.5 What additional equipment and backup may be necessary?

In conventional teaching and training contexts, all the equipment, kit and aids are readily at hand. If you are producing self-instructional materials for use in distance or open learning contexts you may have to consider what additional equipment and backup may be necessary; some of these are summarized in Figure 4.9.

Distance learning contexts
- Materials supplied by mail/to be collected?
- Access to: audio/video playback facilities, calculator, slide viewer
- Telephone, fax or email contact points
- Personal tutor or mentor
- Self-help groups
- Residential courses

Open learning contexts
- Multiple copies of materials available
- Access to: audio/video playback facilities, labs, workshops, clinical settings
- Personal tutor or mentor
- Self-help groups
- Academic surgery/troubleshooting

Figure 4.9 *Equipment and backup*

4.5.1 Distance learning contexts

In distance learning contexts students may be studying in a whole variety of places: their own home, a canteen during a lunch break, or on trains, planes and in automobiles. It is highly unlikely that you will be on hand to distribute copies of the teaching material – so how will they get it? Will they collect it from the institution, will it be mailed, sent by courier service or delivered by lorry to a regional centre? Many countries have well-developed postal services, but not all. Open Universities in India and Sri Lanka have hired lorries to take teaching material to regional distribution centres. In Southern Africa institutions have made arrangements with soft drink companies to drop off course materials at trading stores in remote areas of the country. If Coca-Cola can get their bottles to these places you can get your teaching material there as well.

Your teaching package may include audio, video and computer-based materials. Do all students have appropriate playback facilities? Will you provide them for individual use, either at home or in a study centre? If students need to view high-quality images, will they be provided as photographs or slides? If as slides, will students have a slide viewer or will you need to provide one? (If your immediate vision is of a large machine think again. Small plastic hand-held viewers are available for a few pence – viewers that pack flat and which can be assembled by the student.) Will students need calculators, stopwatches, chemicals and apparatus? Your surveys may indicate that all students either own or have access to a calculator or digital watch. You may decide, like the Society of Cosmetic Scientists, to send previously weighed amounts of chemicals to students so that they could make up to the correct concentrations. You may also decide that costly chemical apparatus is not necessary for students to conduct experiments and to witness the main reactions or principles involved. Everyday items of crockery may enable them to demonstrate the principles just as well as expensive glassware.

Conventional students typically have ready access to teachers and trainers in the course of teaching, and personal tutors, line managers or mentors outside scheduled sessions. How will your learners make contact with you if they are in need of help, if they are stuck? Will you operate a telephone or fax hot-line, with colleagues responding according to a rota? Will you organize students into self-help groups, where they can give mutual support? Will you offer weekend activities or residential schools? Will students be able to contact you via email?

4.5.2 Open learning contexts

Teaching and training in open learning contexts are extremely varied. Students may attend the institution and work independently or take part in group activities. If they are working independently, on- or off-site, what additional equipment and backup will they need? Many of those identified for distance learning contexts (Figure 4.9) may apply.

Students may still need their own personal copies of the teaching material or they may be able to share multiple copies that are provided in a library or other location. Similarly, audio/video playback equipment, apparatus, kit and models may be available in carrels or workstations in labs, workshops or clinical settings.

Personal tutors and mentors may compensate for the lack of regular personal contact. Regular academic surgeries or optional tutorials may be offered. There is certainly no reason why self-help groups should not be organized.

References

Freeman, R (1997) *Managing Open Systems*, Kogan Page, London.
Rowntree, D (1992) *Exploring Open and Distance Learning*, Kogan Page, London.
Society of Cosmetic Scientists (1995) *Distance Learning Course*, Society of Cosmetic Scientists, Delaport House, 57 Guildford Street, Luton LU1 2NL.

Chapter 5

Target audience

Teachers, trainers and administrators invariably build up a picture of the group of individuals who will form the next cohort of a course or who will be attracted to a new course. But how much do you actually know about these target audiences, in terms of their:

- demographic characteristics
- level of education, qualifications and experience
- expectations – hopes and fears (and those of their employers)
- interests, hobbies and time available for study
- study skills and motivation to study self-instructional material
- numbers likely to register for the course?

Could you write a general description of your typical learner, or even a detailed profile? Is there a published description of the characteristics of the students following your course or one for those people you expect to be attracted to a new course? If so, when was it written or updated, how accurate is it and where does it appear?

In Figure 5.1 is an example that Derek Rowntree (Rowntree, 1994) offered when talking about the profile of a typical learner. While it is unlikely that you will have dozens of learners who match this profile, it can be useful in creating an image of the audience you have in mind. Presumably your 'consumer survey' will either inform or revise such a profile. In contrast, Figure 5.2 reproduces part of a typical computer printout that provides information on the group of students registered for a particular OU course (Open University, 1997). It reveals where these students live in the UK (by OU region), the proportion of men and women, their age, when they ended full-time education, their qualification on entry to the OU and current qualifications. It indicates their occupation on entry to the OU and current occupation as well as placing them into various categories to aid course administration. It is likely that your institution maintains a similar database that could inform your teaching and course administration by knowing more about your learners.

Profile of the typical learner –
for 'Managing your Farm's Finances'

Our typical* learner runs a small farm or market garden. He is male, between 30 and 40 years of age, and is married with one or two children living at home. He left school at 16 with a few examination certificates and has done no systematic studying since. His most regular reading will be at *Daily Mail* level.

He will not be worried about the cost of books or travelling to course meetings and will be ready to obtain play-back machines for audio- and video-cassettes if he does not have them already. However, he is unwilling to commit himself to attending even occasional class meetings at a fixed time (because of the unpredictable demands of his work). This, in fact, is why he is choosing an open learning course.

He is enrolling for the course in hope of improving his efficiency and profitability and avoiding hassle from his bank manager, accountant and tax inspector. He will be perfectly capable of learning on his own, provided the materials are flexible enough for him to find his own level and he is allowed fairly ready access (at least by telephone) to a tutor or other learners if he gets into difficulties. The tutor will need to be scrupulous in providing support rather than criticism.

Needless to say, the learner is very familiar with the subject-matter of the course. He will be scathing about anything he regards as 'unrealistic' in our examples or suggestions, and will not stick with the course unless it remains clearly relevant to what he perceives as his needs.

*NOTE: Don't expect all learners to be typical – eg a few of those 'hes' may be 'shes'

Rowntree (1994, page 45)

Figure 5.1 *Example of a description of learners*

If you have been teaching a course for several years, you will have built up a picture of the student group and will have planned both the course and method of teaching accordingly. You will have detected whether there has been a change in the characteristics of the students and will have amended the course and teaching methods accordingly. If you are developing a new course, or making an existing course available to a wider audience through the use of self-instructional material, you will need to determine the characteristics of your learners. I would suggest that you have a couple of options open to you, which are not mutually exclusive, depending on whether the workshop on 'target audience' is merely to raise awareness of the need for information about your learners or to design a programme to identify and obtain the specific information you need.

	Course:	M101: Mathematics: A Foundation Course
	Year:	1996
	Presentation:	
	Analysis Date:	17/02/97

	Final	Col %	Passed %
	3157	100	73
UK Regions			
London	336	11	60
South	324	11	74
South West	261	9	79
West Midlands	179	6	71
East Midlands	198	7	77
East Anglia	313	11	76
Yorkshire	206	7	68
North West	225	8	77
North	147	5	80
Wales	120	4	76
Scotland	324	11	73
Ireland	76	3	72
South East	222	8	72
Total UK	2931	100	73
Present Occupation			
Corporate Managers and Administrators	222	8	76
Managers/Proprtrs in Agric & Services	42	2	74
Science and Engineering Professions	62	2	81
Science & Engineering Assoc Profssns	499	19	78
Health Professionals	16	1	81
Health Associate Professionals	40	2	75
Teaching Professionals in School	48	2	85
Teaching Professionals in FE and HE	26	1	81
Other Teaching Professions	18	1	94
Other Professionals	35	1	69
Other Associate Professionals	78	3	71
Clerical Occupations	219	8	81
Secretarial Occupations	47	2	64
Skilled Construction Trades	16	1	81
Skilled Engineering Trades	372	14	73
Other Skilled Trades	75	3	68
Security and Protection Occupations	216	8	75
Personal Service Occupations	49	2	76

Figure 5.2 *Example of a course-based analysis of an undergraduate student population*

Buyers, Brokers & Sales Reps	35	1	60
Other Sales Occupations	35	1	63
Industrial Plant & Machine Operators	47	2	66
Drivers and Mobile Machine Operators	20	1	75
Other Occs in Agric, Frstry & Fishing	1	0	100
Other Occupations	50	2	54
Never Had a Paid Job	0	0	–
No Data / Old Codes	380	14	61
Not In Paid Work			
Government employment/training scheme	8	2	75
Unemployed	186	37	63
Unable to work due to health reasons	42	8	74
In full-time education	19	4	58
Unpaid voluntary work	11	2	64
Retired	66	13	71
Looking after home and family	177	35	84
Age			
Under 25	336	11	67
25-29	700	22	75
30-39	1305	41	75
40-49	590	19	71
50-59	148	12	70
60-64	40	1	75
65 and over	38	1	55
Gender			
Male	2445	77	71
Female	712	23	78
Ethnic Origin			
Asian	101	3	63
Black	91	3	49
White	2830	90	75
Other Groups	21	1	62
Invalid/Missing Data	114	4	49
Disability	121	4	69
No Disability	3036	96	73
Educational Qualifications on Entry			
No formal	57	2	47

Figure 5.2 (contd)

CSE, RSA, School Certificate	63	2	48
'O' level (1-4 subjects)	261	8	59
'A' level (1 subject)	134	4	74
ONC/OND	455	14	73
HNC/HND	744	24	81
Teacher's Certificate	46	1	54
University diploma	63	2	70
'O' level (5+ subjects)	306	10	66
University first degree	241	8	77
Postgraduate degree	72	2	67
Professional qual < 'A' level	29	1	48
Professional qual < degree	77	2	64
Professional qual >= degree	86	3	81
'A' level (2+ subjects)	477	15	81
Missing / invalid codes	46	1	54

Figure 5.2 (*contd*)

Option 1
You could look around your institution (and those in which you are in competition) and try to locate published descriptions of the learners following courses – perhaps including a course you teach. Some detective work may reveal how the data was collected, that is the basis of the description, and when it was assembled. A collection of such descriptions could be the starting point of a small group task to review your likely target audience.

Option 2
You could ask a small group of your colleagues to complete a simple quiz (Figure 5.3), to pool their answers, and use this to reveal:

1. how much is known about your learners or prospective learners
2. what else you need to find out
3. what implication this may have for your teaching.

Let's assume you adopt Option 2. The quiz, 'Knowing your learners', could take anything from five minutes to hours to complete. Depending on the time available, you will need to decide whether to circulate it in advance of the workshop, as preparation, or to allocate 15 to 20 minutes to complete it at the start. After completing the quiz, and depending on the number of people attending the workshop and your aim, you could group participants into, say, three groups and ask each one to review the pooled information from one of the three main areas of the quiz – 'Viability of the course', 'Characteristics of the group' and 'Things brought to the course'. You may find it useful to organize the resultant feedback in a matrix (Figure 5.4).

Viability of the course

1. Will the learners be able to afford the course?
    Consider whether the course will be subsidized, must break even or make a profit.
    Consider direct cost (course fees) and indirect costs (course books and equipment).

2. How much time will they have available for study in a typical week?
    Consider the expected average hours of study per week and over what period (months and years) study will be undertaken.

3. Where do the learners live in relation to the teaching/training centre?
    Consider any residential or workplace requirements.
    Consider form of contact with tutors, mentors and supervisors.

4. How many people are likely to register for the course each time it is offered?
    Consider evidence from previous levels of course uptake and whether the target audience is local, regional, national or international.

Characteristics of the group

5. What is the average age of your learners and their range of ages?
    Consider evidence from previous courses.
    Consider how a change in age structure will influence course presentation.

6. What is the ratio of males to females in the group?
    Consider whether domestic and work commitments will influence study and whether the gender balance will affect course presentation.

7. To what race, ethnic or religious group do your learners belong?
    Consider the implications of the course timetable for special religious and cultural events.
    Consider whether some learners may be studying in a second language.

8. What level of education have students completed or what qualifications, if any, have they obtained?
    Consider Accreditation of Prior Learning, the specified course prerequisites and 'currency' of existing qualification.

Things brought to the course

9. What is the present occupation of your learners, if any?
    Consider whether occupational experience will contribute to learning and how it may be drawn upon/utilized.

Figure 5.3 *Quiz – knowing your learners (allow about 10 minutes)*

10. What relevant experience do they have that may contribute to their study?
Consider how previous experience will contribute to learning.

11 What study skills do your learners possess and what will be the starting point of your teaching?
Consider what literal, numerical and organizational skills may be required in study and how they can be provided.

12. What additional information do you need about your learners and how would you obtain it?
Consider arrangements for communication-impaired learners and how physically impaired learners can be aided in their study.

Figure 5.3 *(contd)*

	Viability of the course	**Characteristics of the group**	**Things brought to the course**
1. How much is known about our learners or prospective learners?			
2. What else do we need to find out?			
3. What implications might this have for our teaching?			

Figure 5.4 *Quiz feedback on target audience*

5.1 Viability of the course

5.1.1 Will the learners be able to afford the course?

The financial cost to those wishing to follow your course is obviously a major consideration. Will the cost be subsidized by the institution, and if so at what level?

Does the course have to 'break even', and if so over what period? What additional costs, both direct and indirect, may learners incur? Do you have any evidence as to the effect of take-up on the course in relation to its cost? Furthermore, one of the typical features of open and distance learning materials is that you often incur, or are committed to, a large proportion of the cost of the course before students register and pay their fees or before monies are released!

The Open University, for example, incurs major 'front end' costs on its courses and then charges students for each course they study. While I am sure that many regard the cost of undergraduate courses as high, the price students actually pay is about 20 per cent of the actual cost; the rest is subsidized by the British Government. Are you able to determine what level of subsidy, if any, your institution is prepared to contribute to your course?

If your courses are required to 'break even', or even make a profit, over how many years will the calculation be made? The problem is in balancing the course production budget, and all costs in its delivery, with the estimated student numbers over the life of the course. If you are faced with this problem, the recent book entitled *The Costs and Economics of Open and Distance Learning* (Rumble, 1997) should be required reading. Greville Rumble provides insights into the costing of a course, and course elements, that are outside our everyday budgeting experience.

Of course, the price tag attached to a course may not be the only cost that students will incur. Will they need access to a video playback machine or cassette tape recorder? Will they need to buy books and computer equipment? Will they incur travel expenses to a centre or accommodation and subsistence costs in attending a residential component of the course? Furthermore, while people are studying they cannot be working – earning a living. It may be that students will lose overtime or have to pay a babysitter and so on to study your course.

The Open University offers three courses that combine to form a Masters Degree in Distance Education, taught at a distance. In addition to the course fee of £2,435, at 1999 prices, for each of the three courses – a total of £7305 (the course has to 'break even' or make a profit) – all students are told that they require a PC and communication equipment to download information, utilize the Internet, send emails and participate online with a tutor and other students. A detailed specification of the equipment is provided that indicates both the hardware and software required; it will ensure their participation in the course – but at a cost. Because of different makes and models of machine it is difficult to give a precise figure of the cost of setting up the computer and associated software. However, at 1998 prices the typical cost would be just over £1000. Together with the course fees, but not counting books and other expenses, this represents a sum of about £8500. If students cannot afford this they cannot do the three courses that eventually lead to the MA.

Before launching into the production of a course you would be advised to consider, in addition to what learners want to study, how much they are prepared to pay for it! For example, when the National Association of Clinical Tutors (NACT, 1990) were planning their self-instructional training package they surveyed Clinical Tutors on a whole range of issues associated with the course – the topics they wanted to study, the time they were prepared to devote to study and the price they would be prepared to pay for it. Needless to say, the level of fee that they were prepared to pay varied, but it was possible to identify a figure that the vast majority thought was reasonable. This figure, multiplied by the number of copies the Association expected to sell over five years, gave an indication of the gross returns and a basis for planning. It is worth noting that the resultant figures precluded the provision of video materials – Clinical Tutors were not prepared to pay the level of fee that would permit their inclusion.

A further point to consider in relation to the cost of the course is the cost of courses offered by others. In a visit to an Australian university, academic staff were proudly describing the features of their new MBA course available on the Web. Unfortunately, the sobering fact was that a similar MBA course, also on the Web, was available from Harvard University in the USA – and it was cheaper!

5.1.2 How much time will they have available for study in a typical week?

Institutions are increasingly indicating, in some detail, not only the nature of the work they are expecting from students, but also specifying the study time they expect them to devote to it; such indications are typically part of course validation/accreditation procedures. I would argue that such statements represent the basis of a contract between the institution and the learner. But how long should we expect students to study before they can reasonably expect to be successful? The authors of the Hale Report (University Grants Committee, 1964) calculated the time spent by UK undergraduates on a range of subjects in order to complete their degree. They calculated that full-time students studied, on average, 40 hours per week during term time; it equated to about 2,500 hours. The OU based its part-time workload allocations on this report. It adopted a system that equated an OU degree to 12–14 hours of study time per week, for 32 weeks per year, for 6 years.

Many institutions, in course descriptions, indicate the hours per week that they expect students to spend in part-time study. They typically indicate, like the University of the South Pacific (USP), that students should expect to spend 'about 6 hours per week studying the materials provided during the semester'. These guidelines sound extremely reasonable – as long as personal, work, domestic and leisure commitments allow an average of about one hour per night for study. However, if personal illness, unforeseen work demands, requests from spouse/children/relatives, etc. result in study being abandoned for one night, it means two hours the next night to keep on schedule. If only one course is being studied a student is likely to be able to organize their time and cope with these varied demands. However, if several courses are being studied simultaneously it is much more difficult. Furthermore, if the workload estimates are inaccurate, major problems can emerge (Lockwood et al., 1988).

A typical OU full credit or 60 Credit Accumulation Transfer Scheme (CATS) point course requires, on average, two hours per night of part-time study. This may sound modest, but over a period of months and years it can be difficult to sustain. Furthermore, if you think two hours per night is difficult to sustain you may like to consider the likelihood of students sustaining 20–35 hours per week (4–5 hours per night) on part-time study towards Masters degrees. Courses requiring these amounts of study time are not unusual.

Of course, there is a difference between the study time that institutions specify and how much time students are willing to devote. For example, a study has suggested that students are only able, or prepared, to study for what they consider an appropriate length of time (Vos, 1991). Students in this study adjusted the different components that contributed to their full-time study so that they equated to the total they were prepared to commit – about 40 hours per week. Domestic, work and other commitments will reduce this figure substantially for part-time students.

5.1.3 Where do learners live in relation to the teaching/training centre?

If your teaching is to be at a distance it may be immaterial where the learners live. For example, the Society of Cosmetic Scientists have students studying their predominantly printed based course in South Africa, South America and South Australia; they could be at the South Pole. Practical activity kits, audio and video tapes, and printed modules and books are simply mailed to students. The Open University Masters Degree in Distance Education is available to anyone who satisfies the entry regulations, can pay the fee and can obtain the necessary communication equipment; they can study from anywhere in the world.

Where learners live only becomes an issue if the course requires face-to-face sessions with a teacher, trainer or tutor. However, if these can be substituted by telephone conference calls or communication via email it increases the potential audience for the course to the whole world. It also reduces the cost of the course considerably, since face-to-face sessions, especially residential components, are typically the most expensive part of any course.

5.1.4 How many people are likely to register for the course each time it is offered?

If you were planning to sell toothpaste there is no way you would set up a production system, publicize the product, etc without ensuring that there was a market for the toothpaste. The current educational and training climate is similar. Before embarking on the production of your course you have to be certain that there are sufficient people, prepared to pay the fee, to make it viable over a number of years.

If a similar course has been in existence a number of years you have an indicator of the likely market. You may even have the names and addresses of people who have studied with you and who may be interested in a further course – you may already have an immediate course population. However, if the course is offered in a self-instructional format will this increase or decrease these numbers? You could survey existing and former students on your course and get their reactions to following the course at a distance or you could mount a special survey in a selected area.

The danger, of course, is in enthusiastic individuals persuading institutions to commit tens of thousands, if not hundreds of thousands, of pounds to a course that doesn't attract learners. For example, in a recent conference presentation a university teacher from New Zealand described an elaborate multimedia course, taught via the Internet, in his specialist area. The communication system, graphic displays, animation and general use of media was impressive – so was the academic content. Unfortunately, in the 'question time' at the end of the presentation the teacher was asked how many students were following the course. After an embarrassing pause we were told '...three, but unfortunately one of these has dropped out'. This is very expensive course production – so expensive as to be in danger of bankrupting the department, if not the institution.

Before embarking on the design of a new course you may be advised to survey existing databases to discover what existing courses are available *at a distance*. The International Centre for Distance Learning (ICDL) database (http://www-icdl.open.ac.uk) contains details for over 33,000 courses that are available from about 1000 institutions in over 100 countries. It may be a smart move to find out what is already available before assembling your own course – or confirming there is an unfulfilled need.

5.2 Characteristics of the group

5.2.1 What is the average age of your learners and their range of ages?

You may recruit a relatively homogeneous group in terms of age, such as students beginning a college course after leaving school. However, increasingly the need for retraining and more open access to courses has resulted in a widening in the age range of learners. If so, what implications will this have on your course? Will students be more mature? Will they have an academic or technical background that you can exploit or one that may be deficient? Will the actual age of learners have any influence on their performance?

Depending on the age of your learners some events may or may not have occurred in their lifetime and may not be common knowledge. For example, if I mention two ships, the *Torrey Canyon* and the *Amoco Cadiz*, what immediately springs to mind? Both were oil tankers that ran aground and caused major environmental damage. Depending upon their age, it is likely that your students will have heard of the *Amoco Cadiz* because it is fairly recent – the *Torrey Canyon* went aground over 30 years ago! It may be that the examples that you offer and the procedures that you use will be influenced by the age of the learners.

In the paragraph above I asked 'will the actual age of learners have any influence on their performance?' It is interesting to note that in a study that monitored the performance of 'younger' students (those between 18 and 21 years of age) at the OU (Woodley and McIntosh, 1980) it was established that in general they performed less well than more mature students on virtually every course and every level.

5.2.2 What is the ratio of males to females in the group?

If there is evidence that differences in the age of learners are reflected in their course performance, does the gender of learners make any difference? Trends identified within the OU indicate that, in general, women tend to perform better in every subject and at every level than men. In Evans (1994) the influence of gender was a major theme. He argues that we need to recognize gender concerns and the power and depth of masculine and feminine meaning and practice. Evans argues that our sensitivity to gender should be far more than working towards a balance in the sexes or to being alert to sexist language. Depending on the age of your learners there may be a high proportion of your learners with greater responsibility for child care. Could this influence their availability for tutorials, field courses or residential courses? While many women may find study at home the only available option, it is likely to be on top of an already heavy and demanding domestic workload. Support for such learners, within the family and by the institution, is likely to be critical.

5.2.3 To what race, ethnic or religious group do your learners belong?

Do you have any evidence or suspicion that the race, ethnic or religious group to which your learners belong is likely to have any influence on their study of your course? You may adopt a standpoint that all the students are equal, they follow the same course, have the same opportunities and should be treated exactly the same. While this is egalitarian, it may ignore groups of learners who may be at risk or who observe various cultural and religious practices that could run counter to your plans. For example, in devout Moslem countries videoconference calls or computer-mediated communication links are seldom arranged for a Friday lunchtime or early afternoon; it could clash with prayers.

Within the OU an Action Plan, to monitor access and equal opportunities, has been in operation since 1990. Among the questions added to the OU Application Form were several relating to the students' ethnic origin which have allowed us to monitor the performance of different groups of students over a number of years (Woodley and Ashby, 1994) The findings confirmed that black men were twice as likely to be unemployed as white men – if this were the case with your learners, would this be an important consideration? Would study of the course be dependent upon work-based exercises? The study by Alan Woodley also revealed that on the Technology Foundation course, for example, black students did, in general, do less well than Asian students, who in turn did less well than white students. Could this identify students who are at risk – perhaps by having to study in a second language?

5.2.4 What level of education have students completed or what qualifications, if any, have they obtained?

Common sense would suggest that those with a higher level of education, perhaps indicated by the qualifications they have obtained, will be more successful than those with lesser qualifications. Two of my colleagues within the Institute of Educational Technology Student Research Centre (Ashby and Tomkins, 1996) have reported that to successfully complete their course those students with lower educational qualifications had a significantly higher workload. High workload makes demands not only on their study but on other aspects of their life. This doesn't mean that they will be unable to benefit from the course and successfully complete it, but they are likely to have to work harder than others.

It is not unusual for institutions to specify prerequisites for entry onto their courses. For example, students may require a first degree, several years of experience as a mechanic working on heavy goods vehicles, experience in different areas of nursing or whatever. However, you may attract learners with considerable experience and skill but without formal qualifications. You may attract learners who obtained the qualification 20 or more years ago and who may satisfy your regulations but not your expectations.

5.3 Things brought to the course

5.3.1 What is the present occupation of your learners, if any?

If your course population is relatively homogeneous – school leavers or company staff involved in periodic updating courses – you may have fewer problems predicting the starting point of your teaching. Note that I say fewer problems rather than no problems! However, if you are planning to attract mature learners from a broad background, knowledge of their occupation is likely to be important. For example, when the multinational company Johnson & Johnson Medical were planning their self-instructional training, based primarily on a CD-ROM, for new sales representatives, they were aware that new recruits could include general practitioners as well as car salespeople. The doctors would be familiar with the medical aspects of the planned training course (vascular access, wound care, etc.) but not with selling techniques (optimum time and place to present products, how to close a deal). Both groups would be unfamiliar with the features of particular products as well as the competition from other products they would face. The navigation through the CD-ROM, and opportunity to skip some sections and focus on others (depending on their own assessment to achieve stated objectives) was a major consideration – as was the language used and depth of explanation provided.

5.3.2 What relevant experience do they have that may contribute to their study?

Experienced teachers and trainers will be aware that learners bring rich and varied experiences to any course. The secret is to provide opportunities where this relevant experience can be drawn upon and shared with others. The boy who helped his father rebuild the classic motor car will have an experience of mechanics and reading electrical diagrams that some apprentices would envy. Twenty years' experience as a shopkeeper is likely to be invaluable on the training course for VAT inspectors. The trouble is – how do you find out about this experience and create opportunities where it can be used? Perhaps a section on the application form could ask for information on hobbies and interests that are relevant to the course in question.

When the OU Institute of Educational Technology was developmentally testing the course EH 221 *Educational Computing*, a small group of learners were assembled who studied the material, annotated the drafts, summarized their comments on questionnaires and attended a debriefing meeting with members of the OU course team. It was immediately apparent that the debriefing was probably the most valuable part of the whole exercise – a time when not only problems but also solutions could be discussed. We had deliberately assembled a group who had a broad background and range of experience in educational computing. Even so, it is refreshing to be told forcibly by a student, who by chance has more knowledge in one specific area than us, that '...you don't know what you are talking about – this is what you should do and this is how to explain it' – and to be convinced that the student was right!

5.3.3 What study skills do your learners possess and what will be the starting point of your teaching?

Are you able to list the study skills that your learners will need to study the course successfully? Is it more than learning from text, audio and video materials? Do you expect them to interpret tables, diagrams, maps, charts, specialist drawings, etc., or to handle samples, manipulate equipment or search databases? You may find it sobering to ask your colleagues how and where they learnt, developed and refined their study skills – assuming you don't just get a puzzled stare! I suspect many will say 'I just picked them up'. These are the successful ones – what about the unsuccessful ones? What if your learners haven't yet 'picked them up' – will they be disadvantaged? Is there a danger that, once into the course, if a problem or deficiency is identified learners will have to divert their attention to acquiring those study skills they need to cope with the teaching and materials? The trouble is, of course, that in many cases the course is like a treadmill: once it starts it doesn't finish until the job is done. Learners who step off the treadmill to acquire the necessary skills find that the wheel has turned several times before they get back onto it – and they are behind! What is more, the effect is cumulative. Two of my colleagues have shown (Macdonald-Ross and Scott, 1995) that when students have poorly developed reading skills, to cope with the materials provided, the effect on workload is significant. Another former colleague (Bates, 1995) argues that just because we watch television and listen to radio doesn't mean we automatically have the skills to learn from these media.

There is no shortage of books that are designed to help students learn to study (Rowntree, 1976) nor of advice and assistance available in Student Support Units. Many institutions, like the OU, even offer prospective learners the chance to assess their own readiness for learning with the opportunity to check their study skills and make good any deficiencies or rustiness. Indeed, this has been the practice of the OU for over 15 years, whereby prospective students receive Preparatory Material several months before their Foundation Course starts. It gives them the opportunity to assess their literacy and numeracy skills, to consider and plan their study environment and to consider the implications for their study on others.

Others maintain that it is possible to identify students at risk by means of their response to questionnaire items designed to assess their approach to study and styles of learning. The Lancaster Inventory is one such instrument (Tait *et al.*, 1995).

5.3.4 What additional information do you need about your learners and how would you obtain it?

Is your course open to all – assuming they can afford it? If learners are blind or partially sighted, can they follow your course? What about the learner who is deaf or in a wheelchair?

Will you have residential components or field trips that will necessitate learners living in a particular country or requiring them to travel great distances?

Will the course require contact with mentors, tutors and supervisors or attachment to a workplace – be it a school, office or factory?

Will learners be volunteers or 'pressed men' – perhaps recommended or funded by an employer? Will sponsorship be associated with pressure to do well – no matter how difficult/demanding the course?

It is likely that your standard application form will collect some of this material. It may be worth enquiring how additional information can be collected and analysed to provide the information you need. It may also be worth enquiring what steps you need to take to conform with the Data Protection Act.

References

Ashby, A and Tomkins, K (1996) *Analysis of study hours per average week based on students' responses to the 1995 Annual Survey of Courses.* Survey Research Centre, Open University Institute of Educational Technology, Internal Report, December.
Bates, A W (1995) *Technology, Open Learning and Distance Education*, Routledge, London.
Evans, T (1994) *Understanding Learners in Open and Distance Education*, Kogan Page, London.
Lockwood, F, Williams, I and Roberts, D (1988) Improving teaching at a distance within the University of the South Pacific, *International Journal of Educational Development*, 8(3), 265–70.
Macdonald-Ross, M and Scott, B (1995) The readability of OU foundation courses. *Open University Institute of Educational Technology, Text & Readers programme, Technical Report 5*, Open University, Milton Keynes.
NACT (1990) *NACT Training Package*, National Association of Clinical Tutors, 6 St Andrews Place, London NW1 4LB.
Open University (1997) *Course Based Analysis of Undergraduate Student Population*, Open University Institute of Educational Technology Student Research Centre.
Rowntree, D (1976) *Learn How to Study*, Macdonald & Co., London.
Rowntree, D (1994) *Preparing materials for Open, Distance and Flexible Learning*, Kogan Page, London.
Rumble, G (1997) *The Costs and Economics of Open and Distance Learning*, Kogan Page, London.
Tait, H, Speth, C and Entwistle, N (1995) Identifying and advising studens with deficient study skills and strategies, in *Improving Student Learning Through Assessment and Evaluation* (ed G Gibbs), The Oxford Centre for Staff Development, Oxford.
University Grants Committee. (1964) *Report of the Committee on University Teaching Methods*, HMSO, London.

Vos, P (1991) Curriculum control of learning processes in higher education. *Proceedings of the 13th International Forum on Higher Education of the European Association for Institutional Research*, Edinburgh.

Woodley, A and Ashby, A (1994) Target audience: assembling a profile of your learners, in *Materials Production in Open and Distance Learning* (ed F Lockwood), Paul Chapman, London.

Woodley, A and McIntosh, N (1980) *The Door Stood Open*, Falmer Press, Lewis.

Chapter 6

Alternative methods of material production

6.1 Introduction

The last 25 years has witnessed an amazing growth in the use of self-instructional materials. Self-study courses, such as those offered by Wolsey Hall in the United Kingdom and other national correspondence colleges around the world, have been available for many years. However, the establishment of the United Kingdom Open University (UKOU) in 1969 marked a significant point in the use of self-instructional material for adults and in the methods of materials production. It developed and refined the practice of assembling a small group of educationalists, with experience of designing self-instructional material, into a course team. The course team model is widely practised and well documented, and has dominated the UKOU production system for over 25 years. However, in many instances this practice is not always possible, appropriate and cost-effective.

Other institutions, within a variety of subject areas and a wide range of academic or technical levels, have developed alternative methods of material production, which I have termed *Personalized Training*, *Workshop-Generated*, *Text Transformation*, *Independent Comments* and *Wrap Around*. This structured seminar gives you and your participants an opportunity to:

- identify examples of self-instructional materials
- describe the main parameters that are likely to influence their production
- describe, illustrate and analyse these models in terms of the extent to which they do offer viable and cost-effective methods of materials production.

The key questions to address can be listed as:

1. Can you list examples of the use of self-instructional material within education, industry, commerce and the social services?
2. What are the main factors or parameters that will influence how the teaching or training material is produced?
3. Can we describe, illustrate and analyse the alternative methods of materials production?

6.2 Can you list examples of the use of self-instructional material within education, industry, commerce and the social services?

With your participants in small groups, and using the headings of Education, Industry, Commerce and the Social Services, you can ask them to try to identify examples where self-instructional materials are currently being used. Depending on the size of the group you can ask participants to consider all four areas or divide them into four small groups and give them one area each. Depending on their experience, varied backgrounds and interests it is likely you will identify sufficient to list on your overhead. In Figure 6.1 I offer three examples under each of the four headings.

Education	Open Schools
	Open Colleges
	Open Universities
Industry	Rover Cars
	British Telecom
	British Steel
Commerce	High Street banks
	Building societies
	Accountants
Social services	Inland Revenue
	Police
	Nursing

Figure 6.1 *Examples of the use of self-instructional material*

6.2.1 Education

The National Extension College (NEC), Cambridge, UK, is pretty close to the concept of an Open School. It provides self-instructional versions of national curriculum course material and make this available on a national and international basis. There are other less well-known institutions, such as the Hounslow Open Learning Unit, which provides school-level teaching material for the children of travellers. In other countries, such as India and Indonesia, there are huge National Open Schools. In India the problems they face are not only related to assembling the teaching material but to making it available in all the major Indian languages! The Open College within the UK was extremely influential in forging links with local providers and promoting the use of self-instructional material. The UKOU, with approximately 200,000 students, may appear large on a national scale. However, many other national Open Universities have been established, with the growth of several of them likely to be spectacular. For example, it has been estimated that the Indira Gandhi National Open University, India, will ultimately enrol 700,000 students. The Sukhothai Thammathirat Open University in Thailand was expected to have 500,000 students and the Radio and Television Universities of China 1,300,000 students by the early 1990s. Open Universities have been established in Holland, Germany, Pakistan, Korea and Japan, with others planned in such widely differing economic contexts as Bangladesh and Singapore.

6.2.2 Industry

Major companies based in the UK, such as Rover Cars, British Telecom and British Steel, use self-instructional material in their technical and managerial training. Indeed, many industrial organizations have formed their own Open Learning Units to combine the best of traditional face-to-face teaching, workshop and laboratory practice with self-instructional material.

6.2.3 Commerce

The major High Street banks, such as the National Westminster Bank and Barclays Bank, use self-instructional material in their training programmes; many have their own Open Learning Units. Building societies and financial houses all employ self-instructional material to train and upgrade their staff.

6.2.4 Social services

Many of us pay income tax and rely upon the advice of tax inspectors to assess our income, calculate our allowances and arrive at the correct tax code. The UK Inland Revenue trains and retrains over 30,000 people a year in its various branches, much of this using self-instructional materials. When the UK police force wished to update over 80,000 police officers on revisions to the Road Traffic Act, 1991, it used self-instructional techniques to do so. When Nurse Educators in the North East of England wanted to provide a course for nurses on how to administer various drugs, they combined conventional clinical teaching with the use of self-instructional material.

The examples and suggestions from your participants will obviously be the focus of any discussion. However, you can always supplement this list with examples drawn from above.

6.3 What are the main factors or parameters that will influence how the teaching or training material is produced?

If the participants in your structured seminar are already in small groups you can pose the above question or rephrase it as:

> If you were charged with the task of assembling some teaching or training material, what are the three, four or five things you would want to know before you started?

I am pretty sure you would get three or four of the factors or parameters listed in Figure 6.2: funds available, production time-scale, contributors, course length, course support available and estimated student numbers. It is highly likely you will get others, which you will need either to treat as an additional parameter or include in one of those outlined below.

- Funds available
- Production time-scale
- Contributors
- Course length
- Course support available
- Estimated student numbers

Figure 6.2 *Major parameters*

6.3.1 Funds available

The funds available for assembling any teaching or training material are always important. With funds you can pay contributors to develop course materials, purchase existing materials or pay for the release of time from other tasks. Without funds you face the prospect of producing everything yourself; in evenings and weekends, on the margins of your time!

6.3.2 Production time-scale

How much time will you have to assemble the self-instructional materials? Will it be weeks, months or years? Will the production time-scale allow you time to discuss successive drafts, conduct a field trial and actually give you time to produce multiple copies and distribute? Will it give you time to clear copyright and assemble an electronic version of the whole materials?

6.3.3 Contributors

Who will be the contributors? Will you produce all the self-instructional material yourself or will you involve others? Will they be working full-time or part-time? Will they be experienced authors or will they need briefing and training in order to assemble the course you want? Will they be paid or unpaid for their contribution? Will they be available when you need them and be able to meet your schedule?

6.3.4 Course length

How much study time, in terms of total hours, will the course represent? Will it be 5, 50 or 500 hours? Will the course have official start and end points, with an expected rate of study? If so, how will this relate to the study time available during the period of the course? Will you need to liaise with other bodies or groups to get the length of course accepted by others?

6.3.5 Course support available

What course support will be available to you and your colleagues? With funds you can employ secretarial and clerical staff to help in the materials production process. If you think this sounds like an extravagance I suggest you think again. Without skilled secretarial and clerical support you may become the most expensive photocopying operator and envelope stuffer in the institution! You may be able to draw upon institutional staff to assist with a whole range of tasks, from assembling databases to collecting course fees.

6.3.6 Estimated student numbers

How many students do you expect will study the course in its first and subsequent presentations? Is this merely a hope, or is it based on reliable data obtained from a Training Needs Analysis or survey of the target population? Is it possible to estimate how many students you need to attract if the course is to be viable, to fulfil the need you have identified or to break even financially?

6.4 Can we describe, illustrate and analyse the alternative methods of materials production?

I would suggest that any description, illustration or analysis of different methods of materials production would benefit from a framework which allowed different examples to be compared. Figure 6.3 offers four major features (Budget, Schedule, Materials and People), and refers to these when considering the different examples. The points under Budget acknowledge the three main costs in any materials production process – the staff costs in materials production, course support costs, and the fixed and variable costs associated with the choice of media utilized.

Budget

- Staff costs in materials production
- Cost of course support
- Fixed and variable media costs

Schedule

- Rapid (days)
- Short-term (weeks)
- Medium term (months)

Materials

- Appropriateness of existing materials
- Development/refinement required
- Ease of generation/creation of materials

People

- Writing ability of teachers/trainers
- Investment in teachers/trainers
- Skill of coordinator, transformer, consultant

Figure 6.3 *Cost-effective methods of materials production*

The Schedule also offers a three-point continuum through rapid (days), short-term (weeks) and medium term (months). The two- to three-year schedule adopted by some UKOU teams is considered too long for the present activity. It is assumed that if you are to be involved in assembling self-instructional material it is likely that you are more likely to be given weeks and months than years.

The points under Materials refer to an assessment of the appropriateness of existing materials, the development or refinement of materials that may be required and the ease (or otherwise) of producing these materials.

The three key questions associated with People refer to the writing ability of those teachers and trainers who will be assembling the material. Do they have any experience in the writing of self-instructional material? How much time, effort and money do you want to invest in your teachers and trainers in enabling them to write such material? Is it cost-effective to spend considerable sums on training when the likelihood of those skills being used again is remote? Would it be more effective if the funds and resources were used to employ a coordinator, transformer or consultant?

The five alternative models of course production will be described, illustrated and analysed in terms of the extent to which they do offer viable alternative methods of materials production. They are termed *Personalized Training, Workshop-Generated, Text Transformation, Independent Commenting* and *Wrap Around*. You may decide to reduce or increase this number – depending on the experience of your participants and the models with which they are familiar.

6.4.1 Personalized training

Personalized training is designed to equip authors with those skills and techniques they need to deploy when planning and producing self-instructional material *at that moment in time when they need them*. Unlike those models that emphasize a front-end loading principle, where the skills and techniques are conveyed at the outset, this approach conveys only those that are needed for authors to progress to the next stage in the process. The model depends upon three critical factors in materials production: coordination and management of the project, adherence to the production schedule and ongoing advice and assistance to authors.

Training is designed to equip authors with those skills and techniques they need to deploy when planning and producing self-instructional material *at that moment in time when they need them*.

For example, National Association of Clinical Tutors.

Budget

- Paid consultant, volunteer authors
- No course support, self-instructional
- Text-based media

Schedule

- Medium term, months

Materials

- Existing and generated material

People

- Investment of authors
- Funding of consultant/trainer

Figure 6.4 *Personalized training*

For example, when the UKOU was asked to provide training for members of the National Association of Clinical Tutors (NACT), who were planning to assemble a self-instructional training package for Clinical Tutors (Clinical Tutors are those senior medical staff who provide the postgraduate medical education for hospital doctors), a personalized form of training was devised. It involved constituting a small task group, devising a realistic schedule in which a member of the UKOU would not only coordinate the whole project but would also provide the personalized training that was necessary for materials production (Figure 6.4)

A task group of six individuals was assembled. It consisted of four authors who had considerable experience as Clinical Tutors but none of writing self-instructional material (these doctors agreed to contribute to the project at the same time as they fulfilled their normal medical and clinical roles in hospital), an educational technologist from the UKOU who had considerable experience of producing self-instructional material, but who did not have a medical background, and a representative from the Joint Centre for Educational Research and Development in Medicine to advise the group and to provide liaison with the Department of Health, which was financially supporting the project. The educational technologist was to act as Task Group coordinator and administrator and be responsible for briefing and training; the four medical representatives were to draft the training material. A detailed course schedule was devised for the production of the training package. It specified the dates of all Task Group meetings, the period allowed for materials production and deadlines, as well as the turn-round time for the circulation of materials if everyone was to be informed prior to the following meeting. On the basis of previous experience of designing similar self-instructional material, and advising and assisting other authors, a series of briefing and training workshops were devised and conducted at the time of Task Group meetings. They were designed to equip authors with the skills and techniques they needed to complete current tasks. A telephone hot-line was instituted for any author in need of immediate advice or assistance; it was used infrequently.

This method of material production may be appropriate when a small budget is available for the task in hand, a short production schedule is envisaged and a training investment in the authors is judged to be worthwhile. The NACT Training Package (NACT, 1990) was assembled on schedule, within the budget and met the training needs that had been identified. The exercise demonstrated that it was possible for a small group of medical specialists, with no previous experience of writing self-instructional material, to be equipped with the necessary skills and techniques at the same time that materials were being produced. The product of the exercise was not only a training package but specialist medical staff who had acquired valuable additional writing skills to be used in other projects at some future time. The part-time authors produced material in a limited time period and which did not require the ongoing support of tutors or mentors; it thus reduced the staff costs considerably. Furthermore, the training materials were entirely print based, thus reducing the fixed and variable costs associated with the media selected for teaching.

6.4.2 Workshop generated

When appropriate teaching material is not available, or doubt is expressed as to its existence, *it can be readily generated in a workshop context by subject matter specialists*. A group of specialist educators, with a specific goal and product in mind, working within a limited time-scale and budget, can pool their experience and expertise to generate a set of teaching materials that would be beyond the resources of a single person. This method of materials production does have similarities with that of course team production, in that it embodies a collective responsibility to the input, but it differs in the speed with which materials are generated and the roles of the subject matter specialists and editor in the project. The workshop-generated process is illustrated by the production of the medical training material *Seeking Standards in Practice – Coronary Heart Disease Prevention in Primary Care* (The Medicine Group, 1991) (Figure 6.5). Medical authorities recognized the need for guidelines for coronary heart disease prevention. Their solution was to organize a residential weekend in which a small group of medical specialists, including general practitioners, a practice nurse, a practice manager, medical educationalists and medical writers (editors) met over a weekend to generate an appropriate training module. Participants attended the weekend workshop and contributed those outlines they had prepared in response to their brief and generated others. Not only were detailed notes taken during the group discussion, with a tape-recorded account made for subsequent review, but summaries of discussion points were agreed and recorded. The intention was to pool the experience and expertise of all the participants and to create a composite of their knowledge. The outcome was a resource package containing a self-instructional booklet of core training material for all medical and administrative staff working within a Coronary Heart Disease Clinic, a series of activities presenting a series of worthwhile tasks to be undertaken by appropriate staff prior to the institution of a Clinic, and resources which provided reference materials or information on how to obtain them.

The workshop-generated model, as a method of materials production, has two attractive features. The first is that it can be obtained extremely quickly. The actual process can be accomplished in hours, even though planning the workshop, assembling detailed briefs, coordinating the input of participants and following up the suggestions and sources made by participants may take several weeks. While the task of the medical writer (editor), to present the pooled information, has similarities to that of an author in a course team, it is completed in days and weeks rather than months and years. The second is that it creates a collaborative rather than competitive environment; asking practitioners to share their experience, skills and abilities with others acknowledges their worth and places them in a context where they feel valued. If the context also provides an opportunity for participants to benefit from the experience, skills and abilities contributed by others – to create a resource for the mutual benefit of colleagues – it fosters a collaborative rather than competitive working environment. It exploits the strengths and expertise of individual contributors, with others responsible for representing the information in a communicable form. It does, however, place a major emphasis upon detailed prior planning, the allocation of briefs and operation of the workshop to a tight schedule and with a particular product in mind. While the cost of providing high-quality residential ac-commodation and subsistence to a group of contributors may appear high, it is neg-ligible when compared with the consultancy or authorship rates that would be incurred in a conventional course team model. This, together with the freestanding nature of the resource pack and absence of tutor or mentor support reduces the staff costs drastically. The sole reliance upon printed material also reduced the fixed and variable media costs to a minimum.

When appropriate teaching material is not available, or doubt is expressed as to its existence, *it can be readily generated in a workshop context by subject matter specialists*.

For example, coronary heart disease prevention in primary care.

Budget

- Paid coordinator, volunteer contributors, hotel bill
- Peer support in health clinic
- Text-based media

Schedule

- Rapid, days

Materials

- Existing and refined material

People

- Pooled experience and expertise
- Funding of coordinator

Figure 6.5 *Workshop generated*

6.4.3 Text transformation

When materials are already in existence, but are considered to be inadequate for their intended purpose, *they can be transformed into high-quality self-instructional material* by the process of text transformation. This process differs fundamentally from the course team process, which typically commences with broad aims and specifies de-tailed objectives, with authors typically remaining responsible for their own mater-ial and its development. The text transformation process typically starts with developed materials. The task is to determine the degree of change that would be ac-ceptable and to differentiate between those changes that are desirable and those that are feasible within the time-scale, acceptable to the original authors and which cost a reasonable amount. The attributes needed by the transformer have been identified and described (Macdonald-Ross and Waller, 1976). More recently, the role of the transformer has been discussed and guidelines for the task and examples of the process provided – focusing on the broad aims of the course and the characteristics of the learners, as well as on the teaching strategies and methods of presentation to be deployed (Melton, 1990).

An example of text transformation that closely resembles the procedures outlined by Melton is provided by the Population Training Programme (POPTRAN), which was originally developed within the Cardiff University Population Centre, UK, in the mid-1980s (Figure 6.6). POPTRAN was originally a computer-assisted learning (CAL) package designed to help users understand more about population statistics and dynamics. It consisted of a series of nine computer simulations of population representations (on disk) and three substantial printed manuals designed to help users explore nearly 200 national populations according to certain parameters. However, an independent review of the package suggested that a series of changes could enhance its teaching effectiveness.

When materials are already in existence, but are considered to be inadequate for their intended purpose, *they can be transformed into high-quality self-instructional material* by the process of text transformation.

For example, Population Training Programme.

Budget

- Paid transformer, cost of revisions
- No course support, self-instructional
- Computer-assisted learning (CAL)

Schedule

- Short-term, weeks

Materials

- Negotiation of revisions

People

- Skilled transformer(s)
- Negotiated product

Figure 6.6 *Text transformation*

Minor changes included the removal of textual duplication, reduction in the number of examples and relocation of technical material to appendices. Moderate changes included the redesign of certain computer graphics, eliminating examples of the computer being used as an *electronic page turner* rather than a machine that could store, retrieve and provide dynamic population displays, and resequencing of the computer programs. Major changes involved a complete reconceptualization of how POPTRAN could be used as a self-instructional package rather than a tutor-led package.

The CAL package, which had taken seven years to develop, was subsequently transformed into an *Introduction and Guide to POPTRAN*, a series of nine computer programs and corresponding *Self-Instruction Guides* and a *Technical Manual* within weeks. Sections of the package were 'mocked up' and piloted in realistic contexts with its overall effectiveness evaluated in field trials (Henderson *et al.*, 1988).

The task of the transformer has similarities with that of the editor described above. Both play a central, influential role in assembling the academic material generated by others. However, while the transformer typically has had no part in assembling the original material, the editor may often be heavily involved. Furthermore, it would be far too limiting to regard text transformation as only a remedial activity, one that salvages existing material. An advantage of this process, it is argued (Lewis and Paine, 1986; Rogers, 1987), is that existing material can be adapted for different teaching purposes and even different audiences. The staff input used in transforming the original materials was a fraction of that previously expended. The self-instructional nature of the CAL programs and manuals dispensed with the need for a tutor or demonstrator. However, while the variable costs of providing printed materials and floppy disks were small, the teaching system depended completely upon access to appropriate computer hardware; a cost that could be significant if an institution had to purchase such hardware merely to run the program(s).

6.4.4 Independent comments

If the characteristics of self-instructional material, *in terms of its academic quality and teaching effectiveness can be identified and agreed*, they can be used as a basis for independent commenting on draft materials. When a group of authors are engaged in the process of transforming their own conventional teaching material into self-instructional material, or creating new teaching material, the constructive comments of an independent specialist can make a significant contribution to the final product. However, the method requires collective agreement on the criteria that identify academic quality and teaching effectiveness and a consistency in terms of the level of detail, advice and assistance provided.

In 1993 the Department of Applied Social Studies, Hong Kong Polytechnic, decided to transform their conventionally taught Diploma in Social Work into an Open Learning course (Hong Kong Polytechnic, 1994). Those aspects of the course that could be taught via self-instructional material would be assembled; tutorials and fieldwork would be retained for those aspects more appropriately taught by face-to-face methods (Figure 6.7).

If the characteristics of effective self-instructional material can be identified and agreed, draft teaching material can be improved by *independent comments* on successive drafts.

For example, Diploma in Social Work

Budget

- Paid consultant, authors from institution
- Self-instructional, authors provide support
- Text-based media

Schedule

- Medium term, months

Materials

- Existing and generated materials
- English a second language for authors and students
- Based on conventional course

People

- Advice and assistance to individuals and group
- Investment in authors
- Quality of advice from consultant

Figure 6.7 *Independent comments*

Academic staff within the department provisionally identified those course objectives most appropriately taught through self-instructional material. At the same time, a series of briefing and training sessions were conducted to identify the characteristics of self-instructional material and the differences between conventional texts and self-instructional texts. Workshops and seminars were conducted to generate the criteria that would identify academic/technical quality and teaching effectiveness; these criteria represented the framework within which all subsequent comments on drafts were assembled.

The task of the independent commentator was to analyse each draft module and return the annotated draft to the author, together with a typewritten report giving general comments on the draft as a whole, comment on the academic/technical quality and teaching effectiveness within the agreed framework as well as specific comments on the text. A combination of periodic meetings between the independent commentator and the authors, letters and audio cassette tapes served to clarify points of misunderstanding or to provide generalized advice and assistance; over 120 two-hour self-instructional modules have been assembled and revised. The briefing and training, together with detailed comments on individual drafts, have resulted in significant improvements in the teaching effectiveness of the material. The self-instructional printed material represents one element within the open learning course. It replaces much of the conventional lecture programme and releases valuable time and resources for tutorial and field work. A factor that has emerged as important is the rapport that is necessary between independent commentators and authors when working together to develop the teaching material.

6.4.5 Wrap around texts

When books, articles and other printed or audiovisual materials are already in existence they can be adopted as core material and *wrap around texts* written to create a self-instructional teaching package. Creating high-quality self-instructional material can be an expensive and time-consuming task, especially if the number of learners is relatively small. If published materials already exist that can be drawn upon, this can offer an extremely effective and efficient way of assembling teaching material, especially if the existing published material represents the vast majority of the study material.

When the Open University decided to produce H521 *Producing an Open Learning Package* (Open University, 1991) it was tempting to assemble teachers and trainers into a course team to pool their expertise and generate a multimedia teaching package. However, attendant time constraints, costs and a limited population of learners made such an approach unacceptable (Figure 6.8).

Fortunately, the Open University was able to identify academic staff who could review existing materials, suggest ways in which they could be supplemented, and identify a member of staff who could assemble the study guide to wrap around the existing materials. The actual production of H521 was based upon a previously published text of 389 pages (Rowntree, 1991) and supplemented by other teaching materials. One of these teaching materials was an audiotape made up of extracts from audiovisual examples: a combination of audiotape with other printed/visual materials (side 1) and specially recorded interviews with individuals who were in the process of assembling self-instructional teaching material (side 2). The other main teaching material took the form of a study guide of 100 pages which referred directly to the published book and to extracts on both sides of the tape. Optional tutorial support was available on request at an additional charge.

H521 *Producing an Open Learning Package* was assembled by a single author in a period of five months – a period which also included piloting the draft material with trainers in industry (trainers who eventually contributed their comments on the audiotape that was part of the teaching package). It represented a quantity of teaching material that would normally have taken a small team of academic staff two years to assemble. The major benefits were that high-quality teaching material could be assembled extremely quickly and at low cost. The major part of the course, the published text, was already in print. Examples of audiovisual material were readily available and other audio materials could be rapidly produced. A pool of experienced tutors were available from within the University.

When books, articles and other printed or audiovisual material are already in existence, they can be adopted as core material and *wrap around texts* written to create a self-instructional package.

For example, Producing an Open Learning Package.

Budget

- Experienced author/coordinator
- Optional tutor support
- Text-based media plus audiovisual material

Schedule

- Medium term, months

Materials

- Existing and generated material

People

- Skilled author, coordinator
  Isolation of author

Figure 6.8 *Wrap around text*

However, although the costs in the present example of a wrap around course were small, the potential costs are worth noting. For example, when using existing materials the producers need to be aware of the copyright implications; copyright costs can be significant. Furthermore, if the assembled package of material is dependent upon a published text, one should ensure that it will continue in print! A second potential cost relates not to materials but to the individual(s) involved – to the pressures upon the author, working alone without the support and encouragement of his colleagues. A great strength of the course team model of materials production is the mutual support that is available as well as the specialist help from particular members of the team. It takes an experienced and confident author to take on the task of assembling, single-handed, a *wrap around* course. Fortunately, in the above example, the Open University was able to call upon Derek Rowntree to assemble the study materials to wrap around his own book. Indeed, the exercise was considered so successful that it is to be repeated in a forthcoming course.

The example illustrates that when existing published materials can be located, and an experienced course developer is available, high-quality wrap around materials can be assembled extremely quickly with extremely low staff costs. Restricting media to print and audiotape reduced variable costs to a minimum.

6.5 Concluding comments

Each of the above methods of materials production has been successfully applied. The key question was to decide, with the resources available and constraints present, which of the methods was possible and appropriate. The decision is influenced by a number of factors: the stage of materials development, the writing abilities of authors, decisions regarding investment in author training and over what period, and the skills of prospective task group coordinator, workshop presenter, text transformer or author.

Given sufficient advance notice, all five methods are possible, although invariably production deadlines are a deciding factor. A major distinction between the process of developing texts and transforming them is the investment that one wishes to make in original authors. If it is unlikely that the author of prospective teaching materials will be involved in similar activities in the future, it may not be cost-effective to invest considerable time, effort and funds in the process; utilizing an experienced transformer may be more appropriate. The availability of specialists may also dictate the method adopted. Contributing to a weekend workshop may be feasible, while a commitment to an arduous production schedule may not. Needless to say, a skilled individual could probably operate all five methods, and combinations of them, successfully.

References

Henderson, E S, Kinzett, S and Lockwood, F G (1988) Developing POPTRAN, a population modelling package, *British Journal of Educational Technology*, **3**, 184–92.

Hong Kong Polytechnic (1994) *Diploma in Social Work*, Department of Applied Social Studies, Hong Kong Polytechnic, Hong Kong.

Lewis, R and Paine, N (1986) *How to find and adapt materials and elect media,* Open Learning Guide 8, Council for Educational Technology, London.

Macdonald-Ross, M and Waller, R (1976) The transformer, in *The Penrose Annual* (eds S Greenwood and C Goodacre), Norwood Publications Ltd, London.

Medicine Group, The (1991) *Seeking Standards in Practice – Coronary Heart Disease Prevention in Primary Care,* The Medicine Group, Oxford

Melton, R F (1990) Transforming text for distance learning, *British Journal of Educational Technology*, **3**, 183–95.

NACT (1990) *NACT Training Package,* National Association of Clinical Tutors, 6 St Andrew's Place, London.

Open University (1991) *Developing an Open Learning Package,* Open University Press, Milton Keynes.

Rogers, W S (1987) Adapting materials for alternative use, in *Open Learning for Adults* (eds M Thorpe and D Grugeon), Longman, Harlow.

Rowntree, D (1991) *Teaching Through Self Instruction*, Kogan Page, London.

Chapter 7

Assembling a course proposal

7.1 Introduction

Before any organization or institution can decide whether to invest time, effort and money in the production of self-instructional materials, it needs a proposal containing a description of the main features of the course, the parameters that are likely to influence its production as well as its characteristics. Without such a document, and associated discussion, you have no idea what is likely to be involved, what will be needed, what will be consumed and what the intended outcome will be.

Assembling a course proposal is often regarded as a formidable task that can take weeks if not months to do. In my experience it is often a time of considerable tension among colleagues as they lurch from one unforeseen problem to another and wallow in a morass of detail as they try to reach a compromise. It is not unusual to hear them talk about the 'racehorse they had in mind that emerged as a camel'!

As an alternative to the protracted and often bitter arguments that typify the assembly of a course proposal I would like to offer something completely different. I'd like to describe a game designed to assemble an outline course proposal in minutes rather than months. With this as a starting point you can then spend more time refining it and making sure you get the racehorse you had in mind. I've played different versions of this game with teachers and trainers in several countries around the world. It is good fun and it works. Indeed, some time ago I played the game with several small groups of staff at The Open Polytechnic of New Zealand, with each group being invited to summarize their discussions and review their proposal. At the time of the review a member of one group stood up and announced that the whole group was thinking of resigning – because they felt the idea they had come up with, and outlined in minutes, was 'a winner', and they 'could make a fortune on this package'.

What I would like to do is explain the materials (board, cards and summary sheet) that you will need, provide an overview of the game and indicate how you could play it with your colleagues. The rules are minimal and merely designed to keep the game moving and to finish on time. Needless to say, you should feel free to *customize* the game to suit your own needs.

7.1.1 Materials needed

You will need a board, or rather a sheet of paper, on which to play the game (Figure 7.1). You can enlarge Figure 7.1 until it is about 420 cm × 594 cm, which is the size of A2. Most photocopiers will allow you to enlarge each half of Figure 7.1 to an A3 sheet, and then you can join them together. I would recommend you aim for between four and six players per board, so you can easily calculate how many boards you will need.

Assembling a course proposal

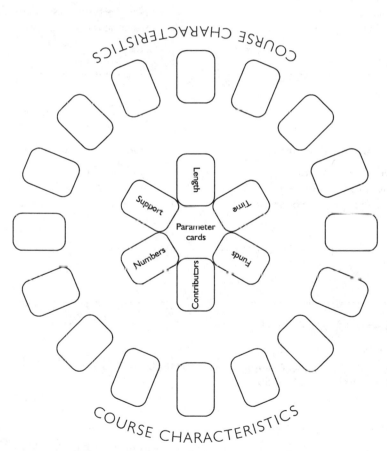

Figure 7.1 *Game board*

Parameter cards for production time-scale

Production time-scale You have 2 months to assemble the course material for handover to production.	**Production time-scale** You have 18 months to assemble the course material for handover to production.
Production time-scale You have 4 months to assemble the course material for handover to production.	**Production time-scale** You have 20 months to assemble the course material for handover to production.
Production time-scale You have 10 months to assemble the course material for handover to production.	**Production time-scale** You have ? months to assemble the course material for handover to production.
Production time-scale You have 12 months to assemble the course material for handover to production.	

Figure 7.2 *Parameter cards*

Parameter cards for course length

Course length

The course will be equivalent to 50 hours of study time.

Course length

The course will be equivalent to 300 hours of study time.

Course length

The course will be equivalent to 100 hours of study time.

Course length

The course will be equivalent to 400 hours of study time.

Course length

The course will be equivalent to 150 hours of study time.

Course length

The course will be equivalent to ? hours of study time.

Course length

The course will be equivalent to 200 hours of study time.

Figure 7.2 (*contd*)

Parameter cards for course support available

Course support available

You have (part-time) one secretary.

Course support available

You have (full-time) one secretary, one administrator, one media adviser and one graphic designer.

Course support available

You have (part-time) one secretary and one administrator.

Course support available

You have (full-time) one secretary, one administrator, one media adviser, one graphic designer and one educational technologist.

Course support available

You have (full-time) one secretary and one administrator.

Course support available

You have the following ?

Course support available

You have (full-time) one secretary, one administrator and one media adviser.

Figure 7.2 (*contd*)

Parameter cards for estimated student numbers

Estimated student numbers

You expect 50 students to study the course each year.

Estimated student numbers

You expect 500 students to study the course each year.

Estimated student numbers

You expect 75 students to study the course each year.

Estimated student numbers

You expect 1000 students to study the course each year.

Estimated student numbers

You expect 150 students to study the course each year.

Estimated student numbers

You expect ? students to study the course each year.

Estimated student numbers

You expect 200 students to study the course each year.

Figure 7.2 (*contd*)

Parameter cards for contributors

<table>
<tr>
<td>

Contributors

You have 1 contributor (part-time) to assemble the course material.

</td>
<td>

Contributors

You have 5 contributors (part-time) to assemble the course material.

</td>
</tr>
<tr>
<td>

Contributors

You have 2 contributors (part-time) to assemble the course material.

</td>
<td>

Contributors

You have 6 contributors (part-time) to assemble the course material.

</td>
</tr>
<tr>
<td>

Contributors

You have 3 contributors (part-time) to assemble the course material.

</td>
<td>

Contributors

You have ? contributors (part-time/full-time) to assemble the course material.

</td>
</tr>
<tr>
<td>

Contributors

You have 4 contributors (part-time) to assemble the course material.

</td>
<td>

</td>
</tr>
</table>

Figure 7.2 (*contd*)

Parameter cards for funds available

Funds available

You have £2,500 available
(excluding salaries) to
assemble the course material.

Funds available

You have £100,000 available
(excluding salaries) to
assemble the course material.

Funds available

You have £5,000 available
(excluding salaries) to
assemble the course material.

Funds available

You have £150,000 available
(excluding salaries) to
assemble the course material.

Funds available

You have £25,000 available
(excluding salaries) to
assemble the course material.

Funds available

You have £? available
(excluding salaries) to
assemble the course material.

Funds available

You have £40,000 available
(excluding salaries) to
assemble the course material.

Figure 7.2 (*contd*)

The sheets of parameter cards (Figure 7.2) can be enlarged to whatever size you feel is appropriate and then copied onto an A4 sheet. I would recommend you copy each of the six sets of parameter cards onto a different coloured paper so as to differentiate between them. It is possible, with care, to position and photocopy the words Funds, Contributors, Numbers, Support, Length and Time (which relate to the main parameters) onto the back of the corresponding sets of coloured sheets and then cut out the individual cards with scissors or a guillotine. A simple alternative is to print sets of sticky labels with the words Funds, Contributors, Numbers, Support, Length and Time and stick these on the reverse side of the parameter cards to indicate which pile is which.

The sheet of course characteristics (Figure 7.3) can also be enlarged to whatever size you feel is appropriate and then copied onto an A4 sheet. To avoid getting the cards mixed up I have found it useful to photocopy the course characteristics cards onto paper of a different colour from the other cards. Finally, you need to cut them into individual cards with scissors or a guillotine. You could reproduce the term 'Course Characteristics' on the back of these cards so that no one confuses the various coloured cards.

To set up the board all you need to do is to place the six sets of parameter cards on their respective spots in the centre of the board – face down. One of the course characteristics cards is placed, face down, on each of the shaded rectangles around the outside of the board. Finally, I would recommend you provide each of the players with an Outline Course Proposal (Figure 7.4), telling them that this is their *aide-mémoire* on which they can summarize their discussions and decisions. With the whole board and cards on a small table you are now ready to start.

7.1.2 Overview

The aim of the game is for players to assemble an Outline Course Proposal (Figure 7.4) and give a brief report on how they intend to realize it – all within 90 minutes. In completing this proposal they will:

- agree the features associated with Course Identification (5 minutes)
- specify or accept the Course Parameters within which the course will be designed (5 minutes)
- discuss the Course Characteristics and decide their relevance to their course proposal ($15 \times 4 = 60$ minutes)
- decide the Method of Production (5 minutes)
- review the proposal and revise any of the previous decisions so as to be consistent (5 minutes)
- report back to the whole group on the outcome of discussions (5 minutes × number of groups).

Course prerequisites

- What skills, abilities and techniques are needed prior to study?
- What courses are excluded combinations?

Target audiences

- What evidence from Training Needs Analyses?
- Will course production be collaborative – if so with whom?

Access and equal opportunities

- How will access by all potential students be ensured?
- Does the course satisfy the Equal Opportunities regs?

Assessment policy

- How will continuous and final assessment be made?
- How will academic and technical competence be monitored?

Needs of the disabled

- Will communication-impaired students be able to study the course?
- What restrictions will physical disability make to study?

Learner support policy

- What plans for tutors/mentor support?
- Will a residential component be part of the course?

Financial cost to students

- What will be the cost of course registration?
- What other costs will be incurred?

Design of course

- What order or sequence alternatives are there in progress through the course?
- Case studies, project work, worked examples available?

Figure 7.3 *Course characteristics.*

Provision of home experiment kit

- Will practical activities be part of the course?
- What safety, pedagogic and cost implications should be considered?

Link to professional body

- Liaison in course construction?
- Negotiations in course accreditation?

Provision of audiovisual media

- What playback facilities are needed?
- Level of access to appropriate equipment?

Further courses available

- Future direction/advice to students?
- Possible course combinations?

Provision of computing resources

- Will computer hardware be provided?
- Will computer software be provided?

Hours of study

- How many hours per week?
- Study to a rigid schedule or flexible?

Reproduction method of materials

- What methods of print production will be adopted?
- Bulk or 'on demand' reproduction?

Figure 7.3 (*contd*)

Course identification

1. Provisional course title

2. Administering department or faculty

3. New course or remake

4. Academic level

5. Date of first presentation

6. Estimated course life

Course parameters

7. Course length

8. Estimated annual student numbers

9. Production time-scale

10. Funds available

11. Contributors

12. Course support available

Method of course production

Figure 7.4 *Outline course proposal*

Course characteristics

13. Course prerequisites
    - *What skills, abilities and techniques are needed prior to study?*
    - *What courses are excluded combinations?*

14. Access and equal opportunities
    - *How will access by all potential students be ensured?*
    - *Does the course satisfy the Equal Opportunities legislation?*

15. Needs of the disabled
    - *Will communication-impaired students be able to study the course?*
    - *What restrictions will physical disability make to study?*

16. Financial cost to students
    - *What will be the cost of course registration?*
    - *What other costs will be incurred?*

17. Target audiences
    - *What evidence from Training Needs Analyses?*
    - *Will course production be collaborative – if so with whom?*

18. Assessment policy
    - *How will continuous and final assessment be made?*
    - *How will academic and technical competence be monitored?*

19. Learner support policy
    - *What plans for tutors/mentor support?*
    - *Will a residential component be part of the course?*

Figure 7.4 (*contd*)

20. Design of course
    - *What order or sequence alternatives are there in progress through the course?*
    - *Case studies, project work, worked examples available?*

21. Provision of a home experiment kit
    - *Will practical activities be part of the course?*
    - *What safety, pedagogic and cost implications should be considered?*

22. Provision of audiovisual media
    - *What playback facilities are needed?*
    - *Level of access to appropriate equipment?*

23. Provision of computing resources
    - *Will computer hardware be provided?*
    - *Will computer software be provided?*

24. Reproduction method of materials
    - *What methods of print production will be adopted?*
    - *Bulk or 'on demand' reproduction?*

25. Link to professional body
    - *Liaison in course construction?*
    - *Negotiations in course accreditation?*

26. Further courses available to students
    - *Future direction/advice to students?*
    - *Possible course combinations?*

27. Hours of study
    - *How many hours per week?*
    - *Study to a rigid schedule or flexible?*

Figure 7.4 (*contd*)

7.1.3 Playing the game and simple rules

I believe it is important that the game be regarded as fun and conducted in a jovial but brisk manner. I have found that it is very easy for players to get side-tracked and to become embroiled in detailed discussion that, while fascinating, is inappropriate to the task of getting an outline proposal together in the time available. As such, I believe it is important that you move between the various groups ensuring that they focus on the topic in question and keep to schedule.

You will have to trust your own judgement as to whether to give all the rules or directions of the game or to reveal them little by little. You will also have to decide how much time to allocate. I have found that it is possible to complete the whole game and have a report back in one hour. However, I feel 90 minutes is more realistic, and does give participants the chance to develop their ideas and arguments without the whole thing becoming too protracted. Below I reveal them stage by stage.

7.1.4 Stage 1 (1 minute)

At the outset it is merely necessary to tell participants that the aim of the game, besides enjoying it, is to assemble an outline course proposal and to complete the document each has been given (Figure 7.4). The problem, for them, is that they do not have weeks – merely minutes! Indeed, the whole game will be played at a brisk pace, with the person conducting it, you, keeping them on schedule with regular time checks. It is worthwhile emphasizing that the proposal *will* be completed in 90 minutes – otherwise the tea, lunch or whatever will be going cold!

Each group is told they are a team who must reach rapid decisions so as to progress the game, even though they will have time to reconsider the implications of earlier decisions at the end. At the outset you should ask one of the players in each group to act as a rapporteur or scribe – to make sure that there is a record of their decisions.

7.1.5 Stage 2 (5 minutes)

Tell the whole group that they have five minutes to decide upon the six course features that are listed under Course Identification, points 1 to 6 (see Figure 7.4). You can refer directly to the figure and merely repeat that, as a group, they have five minutes to decide:

1. Provisional course title	It can be a real course or one dreamed up just for fun. However, the title needs to encapsulate the content and nature of the course.
2. Administering department	To indicate the academic or technical base, the potential links with other bodies and relationship with other courses.
3. New course or remake	Whether a course structure and teaching sequence already exist, along with evaluative data, or if they have to be decided/collected.

4. Academic level	Is the course to be pitched at a diploma, certificate or degree level? Does it result in a qualification at all?
5. Date of first presentation	When the course is to be studied. To fit into a particular term, semester or rolling registration.
6. Estimated course life	From the content and nature of the course, how long is it expected to last before it will become dated and in need of replacement?

Four minute, two minute and one minute warnings, plus comments that they must reach a decision, are usually enough to progress group decisions. Progress can also be maintained if you move from group to group, encouraging them to complete the Outline Course Proposal while reminding them that time is passing.

7.1.6 Stage 3 (5 minutes)

After five minutes you should ask the rapporteur to ensure that he or she has an agreed list of course identifiers and then move on to Course Parameters. At this point it is worth stressing that while many factors influence the design of a course it is impossible in the time available to address them all. As a result, you have identified six which you feel are the main ones (listed in Figure 7.4, points 7 to 12):

7. Course length	How long will it take students to study the course material? Can players estimate this in hours of study time?
8. Estimated annual student numbers	How many students are expected to study the course?
9. Production time-scale	How much time is available to assemble the complete course?
10. Funds available	How much money do you have for the project?
11. Contributors	Who will be the contributors and will these be full-time or part-time?
12. Course support available	What secretarial, administrative, media and instructional design help is available?

You can tell players at this stage that they can either specify each of the six parameters or draw a parameter card to decide for them! If they are assembling a real proposal, as distinct from a fictitious one, they may actually have details of the parameters identified – the course support available, contributors, etc. This information can be written on the blank cards in Figure 7.2. If not, they simply shuffle the corresponding pack of parameter cards and draw one, thus fixing that parameter.

7.1.7 Stage 4 (60 minutes)

After calling 'time', and reminding the rapporteurs to record the decisions of the group on the Outline Course Proposal (Figure 7.4), you should direct players to the Course Characteristics Cards spread around the outside of the board. You could move to one of the groups and invite a player to draw a card. Upon turning it over you should explain that the task of the person who drew that card is to lead a four minute discussion on that topic. You could repeat the prompts on the card and raise others in an attempt to stimulate discussion. For example, if the Course Prerequisites card had been drawn you could ask:

- What skills, abilities, techniques are needed prior to study?
- What courses would be excluded combinations?

and, depending on your knowledge of the course outline they are developing, you could ask:

- What preparatory materials, if any, would be provided before learners commence their studies?
- Will they need access to particular people, equipment, venues, etc?

At the end of the four minutes the group should be agreed as to how this topic relates to the course and how it would be incorporated into their proposal. You should also tell players that after the four minutes are up a different player should draw a card and lead the group discussion on that topic – with the rapporteur recording the decisions or outcome.

7.1.8 Stage 5 (4 minutes)

It is important that you try to keep each of the groups progressing steadily through the game so that when you ask them to review their proposal they have had the opportunity to consider all of the course characteristics. For those groups who 'finish early', you can ask them what other characteristics they could consider that were not listed in Figure 7.4 and reproduced on the cards.

However, prior to the report back to the whole group I would recommend that you give the players a few minutes to review the proposal they have assembled and to make any changes to it they wish.

7.1.9 Stage 6 (5 minutes × number of groups)

You can merely invite the rapporteur, or other member of the group, to describe the main features of their course proposal, its main parameters and course characteristics – and say how they plan to produce it.

7.2 Conclusion

Whenever I play the game I am impressed by the variety of courses that are chosen as the focus of the discussion, how completely people get involved and the speed with which they are able to arrive at sound solutions to the problems facing them. Indeed, it is not unusual for participants to ask whether they can borrow the board, cards, etc. so that they can play the game with their colleagues, or to announce that they intend to work on the proposal and circulate it for approval!

Within 90 minutes it would be ridiculous to say that a full course proposal can be assembled. However, I think you would have a pretty good outline.

Chapter 8

Advance organizers

All academic and technical areas have their own language, technical terms or jargon. The fields of educational technology and open and distance learning are no different. The phrase *advance organizer* is one of these terms; a simple definition is given below (Open University, 1985).

> *Advance organizers* An advance organizer is something which is built into the beginning of a lesson/lecture/module etc. to give the learner a general idea of what is to follow and to help him organize his learning. It can take a number of forms and can be called a number of names. A *contents list*, a *summary* of practical activities, eg 'this lesson will involve you in...', or a statement of *aims and objectives*, can all be used by the student as advance organizers, whether or not that was the primary reason for their inclusion. Any section of learning materials labelled *introduction* or *overview* is usually an advance organizer. The term was coined by Ausubel, an American psychologist.

The following questions are designed to help you consider a number of aspects associated with advance organizers that could contribute to your teaching material.

1. What other advance organizers might you consider incorporating into your self-instructional material?

    (Consider what information, advice and guidelines you might include in any preliminary pages of material.)

2. How would you distinguish between aims and objectives?

    (Consider what they are trying to communicate.)

3. What words and phrases would you use, and which would you avoid, when specifying objectives and why?

   (Consider how you would measure, test or assess the achievement of an objective.)

4. Where would you position aims and objectives in the material and why?

   (Consider not only study of the material but also revision of it.)

5. What are the benefits and costs associated with specifying aims and objectives in self-instructional material?

   (Consider what is specified and how.)

8.1 What other advance organizers might you consider incorporating into your self-instructional material?

The definition above gives several examples of advance organizers: a contents list, a statement of aims and objectives, an introduction, overview or summary. In considering what other advance organizers to incorporate into your self-instructional material you might think about what you would like to know about some teaching material before you start studying it; what would orientate you to the teaching material?

The contents list is a common and obvious one, but what other advance organizers would be useful (see Figure 8.1)? Would a diagrammatic representation of the whole module or course be useful? Would it put the whole teaching material in context and help you find your way around and through it? When the multinational company Johnson & Johnson Medical were assembling their self-instructional training material for new sales representatives they decided to base it on a CD-ROM and to provide, in the CD-ROM, diagrammatic representations that would allow the learners to know precisely where they were in the teaching material at any time (Johnson & Johnson, 1998). The CD-ROM provided a combination of text, incorporating activities and self-test questions, audio clips and video and animation sequences. A main screen (Example 8.1) provided a contents list that allowed the learners to select the module they wanted to study. The modules were free-standing and independent – learners could study them in any sequence. A similar diagrammatic representation at the beginning of each module indicated the content of that module (Example 8.2), while bullet points associated with every screen allowed learners to chart their progress through the material (Example 8.3).

- Contents list
- Diagrammatic representation of module structure
- Time allocations
- Activities/practical tasks/experiments
- Set, recommended or further reading
- Other documents needed – maps, charts, reports
- Equipment needed – calculator, stopwatch, audio or video playback equipment, computer
- Source of advice and assistance
- Key events, dates and deadlines
- Aims and objectives
- Overviews
- Introduction
- Summary
- Assignment

Figure 8.1 *Possible advance organizers*

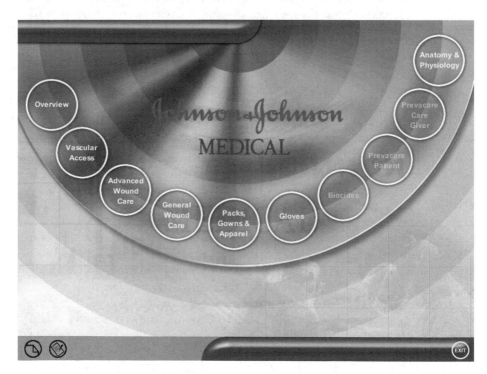

Example 8.1 *Contents of CD-ROM*

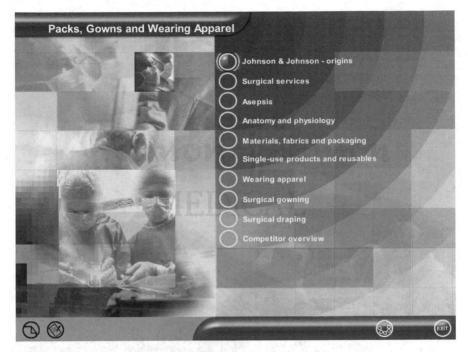

Example 8.2 *Diagrammatic representation of module contents*

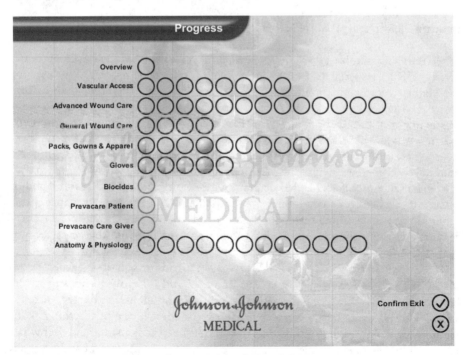

Example 8.2a *Summary of progress through CD-ROM*

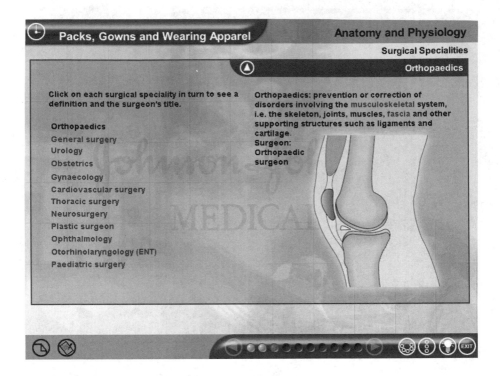

Example 8.3 *Navigation within the CD-ROM*

When the OU assembled *Preparing for the Mathematics Foundation Course* (Open University, 1985b), material that was to be given to every initially registered student on the Mathematics Foundation course so that they could assess their preparedness for study and undertake appropriate work if necessary, a diagrammatic representation was an important advance organizer (see Example 8.4). In a few minutes the student had an overview of what the whole module had to offer and the relationship between the various parts. The group who assembled the mathematics preparatory material combined text with a diagram. Those assembling the technology preparatory material combined a printed diagram with a commentary recorded on audio cassette tape to 'talk the student through' the diagram. Would a diagrammatic representation of your teaching material be a useful advance organizer? Would a representation of the main concepts, ideas, models and theories and the way they are structured in your module help the student orientate themselves to it?

In Chapter 10 the focus is on learner workload – how much time learners have for study and how long materials take to study. Would a useful advance organizer be an indication of how long the various module components are likely to take to study? I suspect that if you were to register for a course, one of the things you would want to know is how much time it would be likely to consume and over what period. The designers of many courses recognize this as important and provide

...you will see that the main route through the package consists of reading Chapters 3, 4, 6, 7 and 9 from this booklet in parallel with reading *Countdown 2* (consisting of Modules 5–9). The top section of the diagram indicates that later in this chapter you will be refereed to the Diagnostic Quiz (which is part of this mailing) and the dotted lines indicate that you may need to refer to *Countdown to Mathematics Volume I* (consisting of Modules 1–4). This is not included in this mailing and we refer to it again later in Chapter 1. The diagram indicates that after reading Chapter 1 and taking the Diagnostic Quiz you could go on to Chapter 2 or Chapter 3 or Chapter 10. The dotted line here indicates an interconnection between Chapters 6 and 10. We should expect most students to read straight through this booklet but there may be good reasons for some people to work in a different way.

Chapter 5 is about tackling Computer Marked Assignments: it follows from Chapters 3 and 4 and makes use of the Assignment Booklet which is part of this mailing. Although Chapter 8 seems to be a dead end it is perhaps one of the more important parts of this booklet. Even if you decide that you do not need to spend a lot of time reading Countdown 2 we think that you should read Chapter 8 quite carefully.

The final two chapters discuss the Open University System (which is described in detail in the *Student handbook*) and the lead in to the Foundation Course. (The Foundation Course is described in the *Course Guide* which you will receive in the first mailing of course material.)

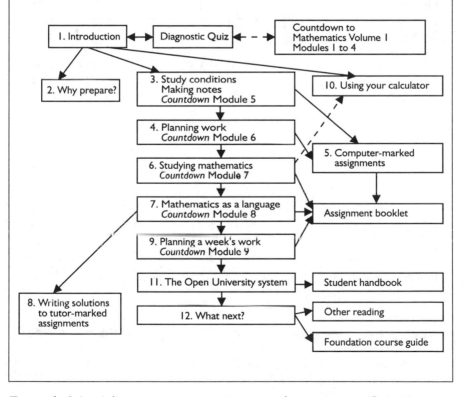

Example 8.4 *A diagrammatic representation as an advance organizer (Open University, 1985b, pages 4–5)*

indicators not only of the time that the whole course is likely to take but the study time associated with individual modules (see Example 8.5). The *time allocation* for the module in Example 8.5 is divided into times for the Main text, Readings, Activities, Broadcasts and Assessment; it indicates an expected study time of about 10 hours – spread over the week. In this example the designers have indicated that in their opinion, presumably based upon their knowledge of the teaching material and experience of previous learners, the Main text is of *moderate difficulty* and the three Readings are judged to be of *moderate difficulty* or *easy*. If you were studying this module, would it be useful to know that Activity No. 7 is likely to take only 10 minutes to complete or that the Miles and Irvine reading, which is judged to be of *moderate difficulty*, is likely to take you 30 minutes? Is it likely that with this advance information you could organize your study more effectively?

Time allocation

Unit component	Estimated level of difficulty[1]	Approximate study time Hours	Minutes
Main text	2		30
Readings			
Miles and Irvine (1980)	2		30
Shaw (1978)	1		30
Campbell (1965)	2		30
Activities			
1			05
2			20
3			10
4			10
5			05
6			10
7			10
8			20
9			10
Broadcasts (including notes)		2	00
Assessment		2	00
Total		10	00

[1]Estimated level of difficulty: 1 = easy; 2 = moderate; 3 = difficult

Example 8.5 *Time allocation as an advance organizer*

Would an early indication of the activities, practical tasks or experiments that are part of the teaching be helpful in organizing the learning of your students? Certainly, in my experience learners can find it extremely frustrating when they settle down to study only to find that they need a particular map, chart, photo, report or whatever – and they don't have it! Similarly, your teaching may involve the use of some equipment – a calculator, stopwatch, or audio or video playback machines. Would it help your learners organize their study if they were alerted to the need for this equipment as early as possible? Advance organizers tend to be associated with the actual material about to be studied. However, you may feel it worthwhile to extend the idea of an advance organizer to the publicity associated with the course. Will students need a computer to study your course? Will they need access to the Internet, a CD player and the software to convert a disk in one format into another? I am sure you can imagine the reaction of students who receive the package of learning materials containing the CD-ROM – only to find that they do not have the software to run it! The phone lines can run hot at times!

In designing your course it is likely that you will decide which of the existing published materials – books, book chapters, poems, articles, extracts, reports, etc. will be a central, integral part of the course and which are interesting but outside the immediate focus of the course. Would it be useful to tell the learners of this distinction? One way you can do this is by grouping the various published materials into a category and giving that category a name. A common division is into *set, recommended* and *further reading*. The actual words used are up to you – as long as the distinction is clear. The following distinction is the one I use. *Set reading* is used to identify material that is a central and integral part of the course – it must be studied if the learner is to have any chance of understanding the ideas, concepts, relationships, implications or whatever that are key parts of the teaching. In practice, you would give the learner a purpose for studying such *set reading*. You would say why it is important and why it is worth reading. You would identify the main ideas or arguments that are presented and pose key questions that would help learners focus their attention. *Recommended reading* refers to those sources that are interesting and worthwhile and which would extend one's understanding of some aspect of the topic in question. However, although interesting it is outside the course and would not be assessed – it is identified as a source of information that the learner can pursue at some future time. In practice, you may provide two or three sentences saying why the reading is worthwhile, what the position taken by the authors is, and the ideas or viewpoint adopted. *Further reading* may be regarded as even further removed from the central course material – essentially a supporting reference.

Example 8.6 illustrates the distinction between set and recommended reading. It also provides examples of other advance organizers – aims and objectives and broadcast components.

Would it be useful for students to know where they can get advice and assistance? When students are stuck they need 'unsticking'. Unfortunately, if your material is being studied away from your lab, workshop, or teaching or seminar room you will not be around to see the puzzled expression. You may not be around to see an arm raised to seek clarification. How you provide this advice and assistance will be up to

Aims
- to describe and analyse the effect of falling roles on contemporary issues in school
- to illustrate how declines in enrolment may influence the character of individual schools
- to consider the complexity of predicting trends in education and the use of forecasts for policy making.

Objectives
By the end of this unit you should be able to:

- identify the major reasons for contemporary changes in the number of pupils attending schools by consideration of:
    the birthrate
    age of compulsory schooling
    staying-on rates
    nursery education policy
    immigration and emigration.
- examine the impact of falling roles on:
    staffing in schools
    school size
    class size
    the teaching profession.
- describe how the impact of trends in school numbers affects discussions on the allocation of resources in education.

Note on reading
There are three set readings associated with this unit, to be found in Reedy, S. and Woodhead, M. (eds) (1980) *Family, Education and Work*, Hodder and Stoughton, London (Reader 1) and Finch, A. and Scrimshaw, P. (eds) (1980) *Standards, Schooling and Education*, Hodder and Stoughton, London (Reader 2). They are:

Miles, L. and Irvine, J. (1980) *Social forecasting; predicting the future or making history?* (Reader 1, Reading 7.2).
Shaw, K (1978) *Managing the curriculum in contraction* (Reader 2, Reading 4.1).
Campbell, W.J. (1965) *School size: its influence on pupils* (Reader 2, Reading 2.4).

Recommended reading
If you wish to read further in this area, you should read:

Husén, T. (1979) *The School in Question*, Oxford University Press, Oxford, Ch. 4.
Briault, E. and Smith, F. (1980) *Falling roles in secondary schools*. National Foundation for Educational Research, Slough.

Broadcast component
Television programme 9 and Radio programme 9 are associated with this unit, both dealing with falling rolls and school closure. You should study the *Broadcast Notes* specifically for these programmes.

Example 8.6   *Collection of advance organizers*

you and the resources available to you and your learners. The Society of Cosmetic Scientists decided to provide advice and assistance via a 'Hot Fax'. If learners were stuck or had a problem they could send a fax to a central number and be assured of a reply within 48 hours – even over weekends and holiday periods. For the third of the students studying outside the UK it was a useful option. Other institutions have organized freephone numbers to an answerphone or have provided office and home telephone numbers in case of problems. Some have operated 'surgeries' where learners can attend at particular times during the week to receive face-to-face help and advice. Depending on the nature of the course and resources available, students may be able to contact you by email; they may even be able to contact fellow learners and form self-help groups as a way of providing mutual support and assistance.

Perhaps one of the simplest and most effective advance organizers is the calendar of key events, dates and deadlines for a course. At a glance your students can see when the next batch of materials is due, the date by which the next assignment must be completed and the date of the final examination – if there is one. The course calendar can flag the times of tutorials, video conference calls, residential schools, field trips, work attachment or factory visits. In an OU survey several years ago, learners were asked about the course calendar and where they put it for easy reference. You might be interested to learn that not only was it highly rated in helping them organize their study, but the most common place for it was on the back of the toilet door – somewhere it would be seen regularly.

An overview, an introduction or summary is sometimes identified by a distinctive typeface, halftone shading or being placed in a box. They are typically highly rated by students as devices that help them orientate themselves to the teaching material. However, perhaps the most widely acknowledged advance organizers are aims and objectives – devices that help both the teacher and the learner.

8.2 How would you distinguish between aims and objectives?

Some years ago I was in an institution that had recently committed itself to the use of self-instructional material in its teaching. I was shown the first module of a new course entitled 'Unit – 1: THE UNIVERSE, THE EARTH, MAN, EVOLUTION AND ORIGINS' and turned to the opening page. At the top of the first page was the following objective for lesson 1.

> To make the student understand the nature and composition of the Universe and also to trace the Origin of life in general and the Origin and development of man in particular.

What is your reaction to this objective? Mine is a mixture of admiration and disbelief; admiration at the scale of such a statement, but disbelief that it could be called an objective. However, my reaction could be due to a difference in understanding between myself and the author as to what constitutes an objective. (By the way, the above objective is from an actual module. I would prefer not to identify it, but if you wanted to undertake some detective work in universities outside the UK you might be able to trace it and confirm the statement.)

If you will be working with colleagues I would urge you to spend some time considering the difference between aims and objectives. In any discussion you could consider characteristics that others have identified and the distinctions they have made between aims and objectives, as illustrated in Examples 8.7 and 8.8.

Aims   An aim, in its special educational sense, is usually a statement, couched in fairly general terms, of what the teacher intends to do during a course or a lesson; it may occasionally be a broad description of what the student is going to do. Some examples might be:

to teach the use of trigonometric tables
to introduce semiconductors
to explain the Otto cycle.
to practise the future tense
to describe cognitive dissonance.

A number of fairly common characteristics can be seen from examples like those given above.

1.   Aims are usually concerned with what the *teacher* is going to do during the lesson; the student's activities, if any, are not often mentioned explicitly.
2.   Aims may express the teacher's intention, but are very far from precise specifications of what is going to take place. They are more like an architect's preliminary sketches than the detailed plans from which a building could be constructed.
3.   Although the learning experience is presumably intended to lead to some desirable outcome, aims rarely make explicit reference to this.

It is true that in some situations the broad and general statements that pass for aims can be a quick and convenient piece of shorthand. Where a group of teachers are in the first stages of designing a whole course, for example, the discussion and refining of aims may be a useful approach to early planning. A more precise form of description is needed, however, as soon as you begin to concern yourself with the details of what is actually going to take place. You need some way of telling your students precisely what they have to do, both during and after the lesson or course. To minimize discontinuities and unnecessary friction, you often need to describe your teaching and learning processes accurately to other teachers too, since teachers take over groups of students from one another and in time, hand them on to yet more teachers. For this sort of communication between teacher, students, and other teachers, a simple statement of aims is not enough. A few examples of the kind of test question which students will be expected to answer, or a set of objectives is needed.

Example 8.7   *Characteristics of aims (Open University, 1985a, pages 6–7)*

Objectives Educational objectives are usually statements designed to identify as clearly as possible what students should do, or be able to do, in order to demonstrate that they have learnt something. Why do we need objectives? Because if we want to know whether we are teaching successfully, we need to have a clear perception of what is to be achieved.

There are considerable advantages in expressing objectives in terms of the knowledge, skills, values, and beliefs that students are expected to acquire from the learning process. We cannot directly observe the accumulation of knowledge or the acquisition of values called for by our objectives, since these are internalized within the individual. We can, however, look for evidence of them by observing the way in which students behave. For this reason, educational objectives are stated as far as possible in terms of what students should be able to do at the end of the learning process. This is of particular important in distance education.

Here is an example of the way in which a fairly specific statement of objectives can be used to clarify a broadly expressed aim (adapted from an OU course):

The overall aim of this unit has been to help you make the first step in understanding how science works. This is why we have chosen everyday observations as the factual material and for our discussion. Having studied the unit, you should appreciate how a simple scientific model is derived from observations, how predictions can be made on the basis of this model, and how and why such predictions are tested by new observations and experiments.

Some more specific aspects of this overall aim are listed below as more detailed objectives. You should be able to:

1. describe the motion of the Earth around the Sun
2. describe the motion of the Moon with respect to the Earth and the Sun
3. give reasons for local variations of the seasonal cycle
4. give reasons for the phases of the Moon.
Etc, etc.

Different teachers starting from the same aim might well produce a somewhat different set of objectives, but the important point is that this particular course team has tried to make clear to the students what they are expected to do on completion of their studies.

Example 8.8   *Characteristics of objectives (Open University, 1985a, pages 121–2)*

The widely accepted distinction is that aims are fairly general and related to what the teacher plans to do, whereas the objectives are specific and relate to what the learner must be able to do. Some people go further and insist that the objective must stipulate precisely what the learner must be able to do, the conditions under which it is done, the level of performance that will be accepted and the time or attempts within which it must be accomplished. The classic book by Robert Mager (Mager, 1990) adopted this position and was probably the most influential book in a generation in the area of aims and objectives. A more recent book (Melton, 1997) takes a softer, more flexible line and suggests that objectives involve judgement and need not be mechanical statements with no room for manoeuvre. The book by Derek Rowntree

(Rowntree, 1994) provides examples of different types of aims and objectives as well as additional sources of information.

8.3 What words and phrases would you use, and which would you avoid, when specifying objectives and why?

If you are trying to specify, as precisely as possible, what you want your learners to be able to do, it is likely you will be employing active verbs – words and phrases listed on the left-hand side of Figure 8.2. For example, you could ask your learners to state Boyle's Law, to distinguish between capitalist and socialist economic theories or represent the decision-making process in granting a bank overdraft diagrammatically. For whatever objective you assemble, learners should be able to determine whether they are able to achieve it after studying the corresponding teaching material. You should be able to measure or quantify their performance.

In contrast the words and phrases on the right-hand side of Figure 8.2, although they sound very grand, are extremely difficult to measure. It is extremely difficult, if not impossible, for learners to be able to judge whether they have achieved the objective if they are stated in terms using these words and phrases. For example, if an 'objective' were to state that the learner 'would appreciate classical music', how would learners demonstrate their learning? How would they demonstrate that they 'appreciated classical music'? Of course, if you rephrased the objective in terms of:

- the learner attending, voluntarily, at least one classic recital in a year
- purchasing at least one audiotape or CD of classical music for their own listening pleasure
- tuning to classical music on the radio more often that tuning to popular music
- being able to compare the compositions of Mozart and Haydn symphonies in relation to the use of woodwind instruments

then it is likely that their learning could be demonstrated and performance measured.

8.4 Where would you position aims and objectives in the material and why?

Statements of aims and objectives have to be positioned somewhere. Even on a CD-ROM, with numerous hypertext links, there has to be a place where they are provided so that learners can access them. In conventional printed material there are several alternatives; two of these are offered in Figure 8.3.

Words and phrases to use	Words and phrases to avoid
State	Know
Describe	Really know
Explain	Understand
List (reasons for)	Really understand
Evaluate	Fully understand
Identify	Be familiar with
Distinguish between	Become acquainted with
Analyse	Have a working knowledge of
Outline arguments for	Acquire a feeling for
Summarize	Appreciate
Represent diagrammatically	Fully appreciate
Compare	Realize the significance of
Recognize	Be aware of
Apply	Have information about
Order reasons for	Believe
Give examples of	Be interested in
Recall	Have a good grasp of
Assess	Develop an intense feeling for
Contrast	

Figure 8.2 *Phrasing objectives*

Model 1: Aims and objectives assembled at the start of each module

- Advantages — Convenient for those who wish to review the content
  Convenient when returning to the material at some future time

- Disadvantages — Presentation of objectives may parade an intimidating list of terms and procedures with which learners are not yet familiar
  A list may be interpreted as prescriptive, limited or authoritarian

Model 2: Aims at the beginning but objectives listed at the end

- Advantages — Learners aware of the general direction but not intimidated by details
  Able to regard the objectives as a checklist when study complete

- Disadvantages — Learners may be unaware of their ability or inability to perform the as-yet unseen objectives
  Objectives may be ignored if placed at the end

Figure 8.3 *Position of aims and objectives*

You could assemble the aims and objectives at the start of each module as in Example 8.6. The advantages are that it is convenient for those who wish to review the content of the module and who may wish to return to it at some future time. It does offer a valuable advance organizer. However, there are disadvantages to this arrangement. The effect of being suddenly faced by a long list of objectives, including terms, ideas and concepts that are new, could be intimidating. Furthermore, the learner may regard the list as all that needs to be studied; a limited list.

Model 2 offers different advantages and disadvantages. By placing the aim at the beginning of the teaching material the overall direction is clear, but the learner isn't intimidated by the details. By placing the objectives at the end of the module they become a checklist. However, there is always the danger that they will be ignored or that learners will be submitted to the teaching irrespective of whether they need it or not.

Needless to say, there are other alternatives. The objectives could be interspersed in the teaching material – clusters of objectives placed at the end of particular sections. Those objectives that are considered essential could be flagged in some way (a different colour, typeface or icon) and differentiated from other objectives considered optional. Particular objectives could be cross-referenced to certain activities, sections or places in the teaching material where they are realized.

8.5 What are the benefits and costs associated with specifying aims and objectives in self-instructional material?

Clear statements of aims and objectives contribute to clear teaching and orientate the learners to the material. They also enable colleagues to communicate with each other and with learners with less chance of misunderstanding. The objectives di-

---

Benefits
- Orientate learners
- Clear statements contribute to clear teaching
- Realize objectives through activities and project work
- An aid to planning and communication between colleagues
- Learners able to monitor progress and check competence
- Able to focus on key areas and avoid misunderstanding

Costs
- Carefully worded objectives are difficult to specify
- Simple objectives may be easy to state but a trivial part of the teaching
- Complex objectives may be open to different interpretations

---

Figure 8.4 *Benefits and costs*

rectly influence the creation of activities – they realize the objectives. By referring to objectives, learners can monitor their progress and check their understanding.

The problem is that drafting carefully worded objectives is not easy. Trivial objectives are often easy to state – but the more complex ones difficult to formulate. The benefits and costs of using aims and objectives are listed in Figure 8.4.

References

Johnson & Johnson (1998) *Medical Representative Training Course*, Johnson & Johnson Ltd, Ascot, UK.

Mager, R (1990) *Preparing Instructional Objectives*, Kogan Page, London.

Melton, R (1997) *Objectives, Competencies and Learning Outcomes*, Kogan Page, London.

Open University (1985a) *P514 Making Self-Instructional Materials for Adults*, Open University Press, Milton Keynes.

Open University (1985b) *Preparing for the Mathematics Foundation Course*, Open University Press, Milton Keynes.

Rowntree, D (1994) *Preparing Materials for Open, Distance and Flexible Learning*, Kogan Page, London.

Chapter 9

Student learning activities

Activities are a characteristic of self-instructional materials. An inspection of any teaching material, from anywhere in the world, will reveal their presence; it will also identify them by a number of terms. They are called exercises, Self-Assessment Questions (SAQs) and also In-Text Questions (ITQs). By the way, there is even a debate as to the difference between an SAQ and an ITQ. In the USA you are likely to find them called Adjunct Aids or even Mathemagenic Devices! This latter term was coined by Ernst Rothkoft, an American researcher (Rothkopf, 1970, page 325); it

> ...is derived from the Greek root *mathemain* – that which is learned – and *gignesthai* – to be born. Mathemagenic behaviors are behaviors that give birth to learning.

In this chapter I have used the general term *activity*. The following questions should help you to consider why and how to incorporate them in your teaching.

1. Why do we need activities in our self-instructional teaching material?
   (Note the reasons that you think are important.)

2. What models influence how we produce them?
   (Consider the influence of Rowntree's 'Tutorial-in-Print' and other models.)

3. What forms can activities take and what problems could be associated with different forms?
   (Consider icons and typographical features, layout and design, space and time allocated.)

4. How do you think activities are used by learners?
    (Speculate from your own experience.)

5. How can you influence learner use?
    (What would encourage you to complete activities?)

9.1 Why do we need activities in our self-instructional teaching material?

Figure 9.1 summarizes the responses that have been obtained from teachers and trainers when they have considered Question 1; the list is illustrative, not exhaustive. It is likely that in your discussions other reasons will be given – but I would expect many of those listed to emerge and be accepted as valid.

To help learners:

- think for themselves
- come up with explanations/solutions
- sort out the features of an argument
- draw inferences
- relate own ideas and experience to topic
- engage in controversy.

To provide opportunities for learners to:

- be exposed to competing ideas and views
- experience those tasks that are typical of the subject
- practice important objectives
- monitor progress
- check their understanding
- reflect on implications of their learning
- actively use the material

Figure 9.1 *Why do we need activities in our self-instructional teaching material?*

Common reasons for the inclusion of activities in self-instructional material are to get students to think for themselves. When learners are posed a question or problem they can come up with their own explanation or their own solutions. The inclusion of activities can help learners to sort out the features of an argument, to draw inferences and to relate their own ideas and experiences to the topic under consideration. In this context teachers have often remarked that in the area of study there are different ideas, opposing theories, alternative models, techniques and so on; they want students to realize they are in this arena and need to be aware of and be engaged in the controversy. In every area of study there are differences of opinion, approach and interpretation. This can range from the extent to which the possible side-effects of drugs, compared with their beneficial affects, can be permitted in clinical pharmacy, to balancing the cost of building materials against the expected life span of the construction in quantity surveying. Indeed, it is not unusual to hear teachers and trainers say '...I'm really not bothered which answer they come up with – as long as they have thought about it and can justify their solution. I want them to realize there are different ways of doing it – many of which are valid'.

Activities provide opportunities for students to be exposed to competing ideas and views that challenge their beliefs, attitudes and practices and to engage in the tasks that are typical of the subject – be this interpreting an X-ray or a wiring diagram, examining rock samples or smelling the constituents of perfumes. However, perhaps the central and most important opportunity that activities provide is to practise important objectives. Whatever the objectives specified in the teaching or training material, the activities are the mechanism that allows students to demonstrate their learning. In doing so learners can monitor their own progress, check their understanding and reflect on the implications of their learning.

At the bottom of Figure 9.1 is the phrase 'To actively use the material'. All the previous suggestions or reasons for the inclusion of activities in self-instructional material culminate in this phrase. If the learning is to be successful, the learners must be involved – they cannot be passive onlookers.

9.2 What models influence how we produce them?

In Question 2 I suggested you consider Rowntree's *Tutorial-in-Print* – and other models. If you are familiar with the Tutorial-in-Print model you can skip the next section and move to the second model – Reflective Action Guide. If not, the following two quotes from Derek Rowntree and subsequent comments and illustrations, should give you the basis of it. The age of the quotes will also indicate that the ideas have been around for a long time; the model is still very influential.

9.2.1 Tutorial-in-Print

These 'tutorials-in-print' stimulate a dialogue between tutor and student, with frequent requests for the student to make a personal response and the author then continuing with a discussion of possible answers and where they might lead (Rowntree, 1974, page 119).

This is why activities... questions, tasks, exercises... are a vital feature of self-instructional material... to keep learners purposefully engaged with the materials... such a tutorial is an interaction between tutor and learner. This is what we are trying to simulate in the tutorial-in-print (Rowntree, 1990, page 120).

The main idea behind the concept of a Tutorial-in-Print is deceptively simple. It starts by asking writers to imagine they have a learner in their company for several hours and to describe the ideal form of teaching that would take place if the topic was to be taught as effectively and as efficiently as possible; to consider what the teacher would be doing and what the learner would be doing in this time. Let me ask you: if you had a learner in your company for two hours and wished to teach a concept, a skill or whatever, what would you do and what would you expect your learner to do?

Rowntree argued that if you really were considering the ideal form of teaching it was highly unlikely that you would simply talk *at* the learner for hour after hour; he simply didn't believe this would happen. Instead he thought you would probably regard a one-to-one tutorial as an ideal form of teaching and describe this form of interaction. In such a tutorial, information, source material, procedures, techniques, arguments, research findings, pictures, raw data etc. would be presented, ideas communicated and learners would be asked to respond to a variety of questions. In some cases the actual answer would be provided; in others a commentary or feedback would be provided. In such a context a learner could be asked a whole series of questions – dependent upon the nature of the topic and the form the teaching was to take. The learner could be asked to recall items of information, draw together arguments, justify particular statements, consult other sources, interpret data, compare different interpretations of the same data, work out examples, discuss things with others and perhaps produce something themselves. In short, teachers would expect the exercise of certain study skills by which the learner constructs his or her own picture of the subject and learns to integrate what has just been taught with what had been learnt before the feedback was provided.

Although this model is known widely as the Tutorial-in-Print model, it doesn't have to be restricted to traditionally prepared printed study guides. Activities based on this model can include newspapers and magazines, technical reports, audio and video recordings, maps, charts, diagrams, practical tasks, computer-based training and Web-based pages – in fact, any form of media.

A key feature of the model is that it tries to simulate the situation where the teacher can predict, fairly accurately, the sort of response that a learner is likely to make. It is most appropriate when the topic in question or the body of knowledge can be clearly identified and circumscribed – so that the teacher can prepare an answer to (or commentary on) the activity that represents the feedback or confirmation the learner requires. Of course, if teachers cannot predict, on the basis of their experience, the scope and depth of typical answers it is difficult, if not impossible, to assemble the appropriate feedback, and this model is probably inappropriate. Let me give you a couple of examples of a Tutorial-in-Print in use (see Example 9.1).

Example 9.1 is drawn from The Road Traffic Act, 1991 (Central Planning Unit, 1991), and is drawn from material designed for UK police officers. The photograph vividly illustrates a common incident for those police officers called to road traffic accidents. The text immediately below the photo provides basic information, while the key question – the activity – 'What offences are you thinking about?', is flagged by a question mark. The actual content of this example isn't really important, and it

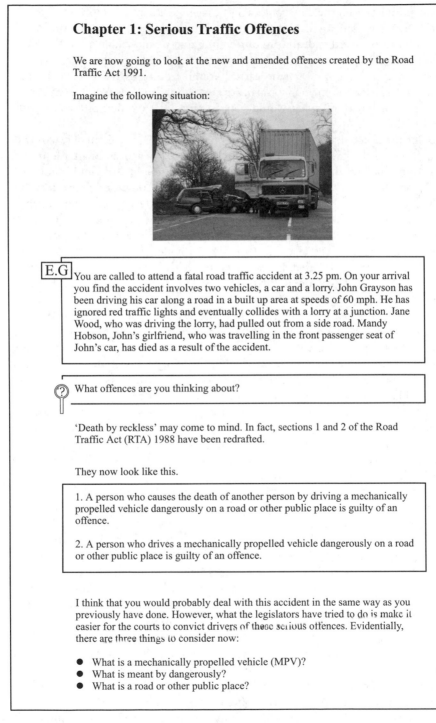

Chapter 1: Serious Traffic Offences

We are now going to look at the new and amended offences created by the Road Traffic Act 1991.

Imagine the following situation:

E.G You are called to attend a fatal road traffic accident at 3.25 pm. On your arrival you find the accident involves two vehicles, a car and a lorry. John Grayson has been driving his car along a road in a built up area at speeds of 60 mph. He has ignored red traffic lights and eventually collides with a lorry at a junction. Jane Wood, who was driving the lorry, had pulled out from a side road. Mandy Hobson, John's girlfriend, who was travelling in the front passenger seat of John's car, has died as a result of the accident.

What offences are you thinking about?

'Death by reckless' may come to mind. In fact, sections 1 and 2 of the Road Traffic Act (RTA) 1988 have been redrafted.

They now look like this.

1. A person who causes the death of another person by driving a mechanically propelled vehicle dangerously on a road or other public place is guilty of an offence.

2. A person who drives a mechanically propelled vehicle dangerously on a road or other public place is guilty of an offence.

I think that you would probably deal with this accident in the same way as you previously have done. However, what the legislators have tried to do is make it easier for the courts to convict drivers of these serious offences. Evidentially, there are three things to consider now:

- What is a mechanically propelled vehicle (MPV)?
- What is meant by dangerously?
- What is a road or other public place?

Example 9.1 *The Road Traffic Act*

will be difficult to appreciate the associated teaching because the example is taken out of context. The point I want to illustrate is that the trainers who provided the photograph, and who posed the question, had a pretty good idea of the offences the learner would be thinking about – hence the comment directly underneath the question. Subsequent material goes on to consider the actual legislation – *the body of knowledge can be clearly identified and circumscribed*; the learner is extremely unlikely to offer answers that differ significantly from those expected.

Example 9.2, 'Effect of elevon position on flight', is from an educational package supplied to children who visit the Science Museum (Science Museum, 1991). The material explains how to assemble the glider and how, with a small piece of plasticine at the nose, the glider can be made to fly. The subsequent text, 'Controlling the flight of the glider', asks what happens if one elevon is raised and the other is lowered; the grid at the foot of Example 9.2 provides a space for observations. These activities are typical of the Tutorial-in-Print model, because the teacher is able to predict pretty accurately what will happen when the positions of the elevons are changed and offer explanations – *the body of knowledge can be clearly identified and circumscribed*. Depending on the type of question, the feedback may also provide examples of plausible but incorrect answers or typical pitfalls, just like you would in a normal face-to-face tutorial.

I'm sure if you consider your own teaching there will be numerous occasions when you set up a teaching situation, and pose questions, with some confidence that you are going to prompt the sort of answer you are looking for.

9.2.2 Reflective Action Guide

If I said that during a course of study much of the important learning could occur outside the self-instructional package, when a learner wasn't actually studying it, I suspect you would agree. If I said the greater proportion of study time devoted to a particular course may take place away from the teaching package you might still agree – but maybe less readily. If I said that during a course of study the nature of the actual activities would be so varied as to make it extremely difficult or even impossible to predict the outcome, I suspect you might begin to feel uneasy. However, this is the situation – where there isn't a clear body of knowledge to be mastered and where independent learning is encouraged – that is at the centre of the concept of the Reflective Action Guide.

Learners have long been equipped with the information and guidelines they need to engage in a learning task away from the classroom, textbook or computer screen. I am sure you can think of examples where learners have been sent off to perform a whole variety of tasks, ranging from scientific field work, collecting survey data via interviews, searching library archives and monitoring the pollution of local streams and rivers to recording noise levels in a locality. However, only comparatively recently has anyone made a clear distinction between those activities that relate to a known 'body of knowledge' and those that relate to 'one's own, unique situation' – to the models of a Tutorial-in-Print and the Reflective Action Guide respectively (Rowntree, 1992).

Fold back the paper or card along the lines so that you can hold the spine underneath the glider.

Stick the model together as shown.

spine

The aircraft is called a delta glider because it is shaped like the Greek letter called delta (Δ).

Try launching the glider. It is likely that it will be too light at the front. Add a piece of Plasticine to the nose of the aircraft, making it easier for the glider to fly through the air. (Do not add too much or it will nose-dive.)

Controlling the flight of the glider

Delta planes like Concorde have elevons that serve as both ailerons and elevators. Make elevons by cutting slits 2 cm long in the positions shown.

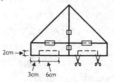

2cm
3cm   6cm

You should now be able to fold the elevons upwards or downwards along the dotted lines.

What happens when both elevons are raised or lowered?

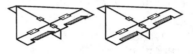

What happens when one elevon is raised while the other is level?

What happens when one is raised and the other is lowered?

Record what you see in a table like the one below.
Try to explain what you see.

Position of elevons		Observations
Right	**Left**	
level	level	
raised	raised	
lowered	lowered	
raised	level	
raised	lowered	

Example 9.2   *Effect of elevon position on flight*

The concept of the Reflective Action Guide is based on several assumptions (see Figure 9.2). A major one is that such activities merely offer advice and guidance to the learners' actions – actions in real and varied contexts, where some skill or ability is developed or refined, and where it is undertaken outside the confines of the study material and which cannot be predicted. This could include farmers determining the balance of cereal crops, livestock and woodland for their own land, trainee managers applying management techniques to their own departments, walkers deciding which route to take between two selected points, and industrial chemists exploring different formulations of a product.

---

1. Activities merely offer advice and guidance to learners' actions – in real and varied contexts
2. Actions performed outside the confines of the printed text – obtaining own resource material
3. Learner involved in reflecting on own learning – thinking critically and setting own parameters
4. Likely to be demanding and time-consuming – related to own unique situation
5. Guidelines and suggestions offered, criteria outlined, but learner to gather and assess feedback.

Figure 9.2 *Reflective Action Guide*

A further feature of activities of the Reflective Action Guide type is that the learner must be involved in thinking critically and reflectively upon his or her actions in order to guide the learning experience. It marks a major distinction between working within known parameters and setting them for oneself.

Another feature is that such activities are often demanding, time-consuming and relate to the unique situation in which the learners find themselves. Finally, resources, guidelines and suggestions can be offered and drawn upon as and when needed; it is virtually impossible to provide feedback that would relate to the outcome of the activity in question. In Example 9.3, the National Coaching Foundation, in conjunction with the Scottish Sports Council, offered self-instructional material on 'Muscle Injuries and Treatment' (Farrally, 1991). It encouraged learners to seek sportsmen and women who had received muscle injuries, and provided a framework in which they could be categorized and guidelines by which the treatment and rates of recovery could be assessed. There was no way the trainer could predict the range and nature of the information collected – but the trainer could give them the framework and the criteria with which to analyse their own learning.

Example 9.4, drawn from *Front of house operations* (Thunhurst, 1990), illustrates how the learner can be given a limited amount of information and then directed away from the study material and to actual 'front of house operations' to discover what facilities or services are offered and what the learner can deduce from this about the clientele. The trainer could not predict whether the learners would visit a caravan park or a guest house, a pub or a hall of residence. However, with the guidelines provided in the teaching the learners could be encouraged to analyse the information they collect and relate this to the overall framework.

ACTIVITY 8

For this activity, you need to talk to two or three people who have suffered recent muscle injuries. If you have been injured recently, you may use yourself as one of the examples.

i   *Find out exactly where in the muscle the injuries were sustained. Check to see if they occurred in different parts of the muscle (for example, some close to the ends of the muscle, others more in the middle).*

SPORT	MUSCLE	LOCATION IN MUSCLE	RECOVERY TIME	TREATMENT RECEIVED

ii   *Find out if there was a difference in recovery time.*
Which location seemed to recover most quickly?
How does this relate to where most of the connective tissue lies in the muscle?

iii   *Your athletes may well have had physiotherapy, especially forms of heat treatment, to help them recover more quickly. Note whether or not they had treatment on the chart. Why should treatment be beneficial?*

iv   *Place a ring around the correct response:*

● *Muscle injuries which occur close to bone are likely to take longer to heal.*   *True/False*

● *Muscle injuries should be treated with ice when they first occur.*   *True/False*

● *Exercising a pulled muscle can speed up the recovery process.*   *True/False*

● *Keeping a muscle warm will speed up the recovery process.*   *True/False*

Example 9.3   *Muscle injuries and treatment*

② THE CUSTOMER

Reception duties in premises offering overnight accommodation vary according to the type of establishment, how busy it is, and the needs of the guests. The mornings and early evenings, when most guests check in and out, tend to be the busiest and if the staff are able to work quickly and efficiently, the customers will be pleased with the quality of service.

Sometimes coach-loads of guests will check in at the same time. Where the establishment has shops, conference and leisure facilities, restaurants and bars, for example, there is likely to be a constant stream of people passing the reception desk and requiring attention.

What guests staying overnight want

What guests want will vary according to the type of establishment and the reasons they are staying there. Often the first contact potential guests have with reception staff is over the telephone, when they will ask whether the facilities they require are available, and at what price. A friendly and informative response from the receptionist could mean the difference between a room filled or a room left vacant.

What overnight guests may want

- room with en suite bathroom
- double, single or twin-bedded room
- bar open until the early hours
- breakfast in bed
- video films
- messages received and passed on
- trained staff available to look after children
- easy access to the room for infirm or wheelchair bound guest
- shoe cleaning, and clothes washing and ironing services or facilities
- room with a view
- orthopaedic bed
- meals available until late
- telephone, radio and television in the room
- clean, tidy room
- early morning call
- choice of continental or English breakfast
- tea and coffee making facilities in room
- choice of newspapers delivered to the room
- family room with cot and extra bed for a child

Tourist or resort hotels The guests will usually be on holiday and will want to relax and enjoy themselves. Many of these hotels have their own leisure facilities such as swimming pools and tennis courts. Friendly and relaxed service to suit the holiday mood does not mean a lower standard of service.

Motels or motor hotels They are mostly patronised by people on business travelling around the country by car. Some may be lonely and want to chat, others will want to get to their rooms as quickly as possible.

Transient hotels These are near a railway station, airport or sea port. Guests will check in and out at all hours of the day and night and may be on edge. Receptionists need to be skilful at avoiding situations which may cause tension and at checking guests out rapidly.

Residential hotels Catering for permanent residents and often called private hotels. A homely atmosphere may be required here.

Business hotels Used mostly by business people for overnight stays and for conferences and other business meetings. Quick and efficient service with good communication services such as telephones and fax machines may be what the customers require. Most establishments are situated in towns and cities where they are easily accessible.

Educational establishments Many universities and colleges provide

4

Example 9.4 *Front of house operations*

9.2.3 Dialogue

Over 30 years ago an author argued that the more explanatory and clear the exposition the less there was for the student to do; that some teaching is so perfect as to stifle all real thinking. He maintained that (Sanders, 1966, page 158):

> If there is an inference to be drawn, the author draws it, and if there is a significant relationship to be noted, the author points it out. There are no loose ends or incomplete analyses... the author does all the thinking. The book never gives a clue that the author pondered (maybe even agonized) over hundreds of decisions. The result is that the creative process and the controversy of competing ideas is hidden from the students.

Ten years ago, when expressing concern about the teaching methods that writers were employing in much self-instructional material, the limiting effect of many teaching materials was again identified. Terry Evans (Evans, 1989, page 117) remarked that:

> I have seen some brilliantly articulated and beautifully illustrated course texts, but they especially can leave the student with a feeling of inadequacy in the face of such perfection, or (even worse) uncritical contentment with having been enlightened.

Evans and fellow writer/researcher Daryl Nation have argued strongly for a greater emphasis upon dialogue in self-instructional material; for the communication that the material generates and the reflective activities that they believe should permeate the whole teaching material. Dialogue involves sharing the thinking of the writer with the learner – to reproduce the form of communication that would take place between teacher and student as well as student and teacher during the process of learning. It does not assume a closed system where the boundaries of students' knowledge are set, questions posed and answers anticipated. The idea is that you're sharing with the learner your own thinking, your own thinking processes.

Examples 9.5 and 9.6 illustrate how dialogue can permeate self-instructional material. In the first (Nunan, 1991), Ted Nunan illustrates how other perspectives can be brought to the topic in question. Nunan represents the three perspectives by three different typefaces: serif for the writer, italic for the student and sanserif for the teacher.

Dialogue has been exploited in teaching texts where the exchange is presented as an 'aside' (Ostwald and Chen, 1993). In their article they liken this to a casual soliloquy (Ostwald and Chen, 1993, page 30):

> It is like the informal introduction to a presentation, or in a Shakespearian sense, when the actor turns towards the audience and delivers a private but insightful reading of the situation purely to allow the audience to understand the scene, and the play continues. It should be noted that the Shakespearian narrator always spoke in the language of the populace, thus it might be seen as a vernacular voice.

Of course, there is always the concern for directing the research activity in distance education to the real needs of the participants – those engaged in teaching at a distance, distance learners, and those who provide services and administer systems which deliver distance education. There is also the further question of whether any special characteristics of the enterprise of distance education shapes, limits, or promotes particular styles of research activity. I believe that my students should be familiar with the developing traditions of research activity within distance education and understand why research is directed towards certain problems. Equally, it is essential to connect research in distance education with the movements in research in education and the social sciences; students should not be constrained by boundaries imposed by current practitioners or researchers in distance education. Students should also be informed of possibilities, techniques and limitations of different, and sometimes competing, research discourses. This enables them to analyse, theorise, and pose questions which deal with a wealth of teaching and learning issues, macro-perspectives involving social and political effects, impacts of distance education systems, communication issues, and indeed, all of the richness of researching a complex entity.

I think I can leave the debate for now; I have the organizing ideas of the area and enough background to be aware of possible criticisms, pitfalls, problems that can arise. What I need now is key resources in each of the three paradigms, as well as some signposts so that I can find my way down particular pathways in the paradigms.

Before we move to the next section, which covers the three paradigms, you may wish to read through the discussions. The discussion on 'Paradigms, ideologies and educational research' is to set the scene for introducing the paradigms; 'Linking theoretical constructs and observations' deals with the way that each paradigm considers the linking of constructs with observation; and 'The nature of research in distance education' considers the types of research activity undertaken in the field.

As well, as a teacher, I wish to acknowledge my debt to the teachers who made up the group that developed course materials to teach about research issues and methods. In writing the materials that follow I have drawn from their resources, discussions and approaches. The preceding story is an adaptation of some of the events that were part of the development of a book, *Issues and Methods of Research* by Helen Connole, Roger Wiseman, Bob Smith and Sandra Speedy. The paper by Ted Nunan in your text, *Research in Distance Education 1*, gives the actual story of the development.

Example 9.5   *Dialogue between writer, student and teacher*

In an introductory sociology course (Sociology 1) I taught recently, I used to begin with a discussion of two competing paradigms [that should send them to the dictionary] of teaching and learning. [Some of them will be aware of these. Some may even be converts!] I don't propose to rehearse that discussion here. If you are not familiar with it perhaps you could ask a fellow student, who has done that course for a lesson. [That should be enough to get the uninitiated enlightened; of course the old hands will learn more explaining to them than they ever did from me. That's why I am a magpie!]

[I'd better not leave the uninitiated completely out on a limb.] Without repeating the discussion in the Sociology 1 course, let me outline the two differing teaching styles which compete for attention in our schools. One can be seen as naturalistic, while the other is technological. The former regards teaching as something which occurs naturally in human interaction; as we do, we teach; as we participate in life, we can learn from our fellow humans and from other parts of nature. The latter regards teaching as a set of techniques; well developed strategies which put things in the sequences that empirical testing has shown to be necessary for effective learning to occur. Each of these is a model; in practice teachers tend to identify with one rather than the other, but to use bits of each. [I wonder if they can pick my own preference.]

You are probably asking yourself [I probably should have said: 'may be asking yourself'], 'When is he going to get to the point? When are we going to find out about the specifics of these teaching methods?' Be patient! Anyway I can't stop you skipping ahead; this is print you know and I'm not there [here?] in the room with you. You may be a student, but you are a free agent.

Example 9.6   *Reflections on an introductory sociology course*

This can be seen in Example 9.6, where Daryl Nation (Nation, 1991, pages 115–16) puts his 'asides' in brackets – to inform the uninitiated. He shared his thinking with the learner.

The three models that often influence the design of activities are not mutually exclusive. When training material was assembled for Clinical Tutors, the medical staff who train doctors (NACT, 1990) the self-instructional material contained activities of both the Tutorial-in-Print and Reflective Action Guide type, as well as incorporating interjections from four 'invented' Clinical Tutors. Example 9.7 illustrates a typical Tutorial-in-Print activity with the interjection made by a fellow Clinical Tutor, the intention being to provoke comment and dialogue, to offer an alternative competing point of view.

1   Introduction

Resource management and clinical budgeting are permeating the NHS at great speed, but cannot be successfully introduced without good financial accounting. If your postgraduate centre (PGC) is anything like mine and countless others, you and your administrator will have found some difficulty filling in the sums for the core module to give you the real costs of running your PGC and its educational activities. This is due to the 'dual' funding of PGCs (DHA and trust funds) and to the way most DHAs lump running costs into district expenses under broad functional headings, eg cleaning, heating, telephone, salaries etc.

Most district finance departments are undergoing a revolution and it seems likely that PGCs will become an identified resource with a budget for all expenses and the clinical tutor as budget holder.

ACTIVITY 1
(allow about five minutes)

Changes in financial management

What do you think are the advantages and disadvantages of becoming a budget holder responsible for all your centre's income and expenses?

Advantages	*Disadvantages*
1	
2	
3	

You may feel it would be dull, too time-consuming and that you are not qualified for the task. It would display your centre's assets for anyone to see and could lead to additional demands on your funds.

On the other hand it would give you the independence and freedom to manage the centre's staff and resources to get best value for money. With adequate support from accountant, treasurer and administrator all sharing out the tasks, the demands on your time can be contained and financial skills rapidly acquired.

> *If we don't get our accounting right and know where the money goes, it must damage our case for more funding.*

Example 9.7   *Changes in financial management*

9.3 What forms can activities take and what problems could be associated with different forms?

The additional advice associated with Question 3 suggested you 'Consider icons and typographical features, layout and design, space and time allocated'.

9.3.1 Icons and typographical features

Common features of activities are the icons and other typographical features used to identify or flag them in the material. There are hundreds of symbols or icons that have been used to denote an activity – from a single question mark to a cluster of them, a hand holding a pen to 'stop' signs, or a representation of Rodin's sculpture 'The Thinker' to 'Men at Work' signs (see Example 9.8). When other media are used as part of an activity it is not unusual to see icons of textbooks, audio and videocassette recorders, TV monitors and microcomputers (see also Example 9.8). I recently saw a CD-ROM that contained 10,000 items of clip art for pasting into teaching or training material – you can be sure there would be dozens of icons that you could choose from to denote your activities. From evidence obtained within the OU it would appear that these icons do perform a valuable function in alerting the learner to the forthcoming activity and to the various media associated with it.

If you can remember the days of Programmed Learning and learning machines you will recall the use of a frieze, border or strip along the page or screen to denote the end of a piece of instruction and to separate the teaching from the assessment material. In the jargon of the time these were called 'student stoppers'. They were intended to stop the student at that particular point in the teaching and get them to engage in some activity. Example 9.8 illustrates just a few of these traditional student stoppers. More recently these exotic friezes have often been replaced by a simple line or band across the page or screen.

However, there are problems with using icons and other typographic features. An icon works when what it symbolizes is immediately apparent, but this is not as easy as you may think; how familiar are you with all the symbols in the Highway Code? This was apparent recently when I was presented with some self-instructional material in the area of coastal navigation. As I flicked through the material I noted an icon of a skull and crossbones – reminiscent of pirates or minefields. My immediate reaction was danger – keep away. In fact, this was the icon that had been selected for the activities – to attract attention!

Judicious use of icons can be extremely efficient in alerting the learner to elements and constituent items in the learner's material. However, there can be a problem in that too many can be daunting and confusing (see Example 9.9). In this OU course (Open University, 1987) there were 26 separate icons used to denote different course components.

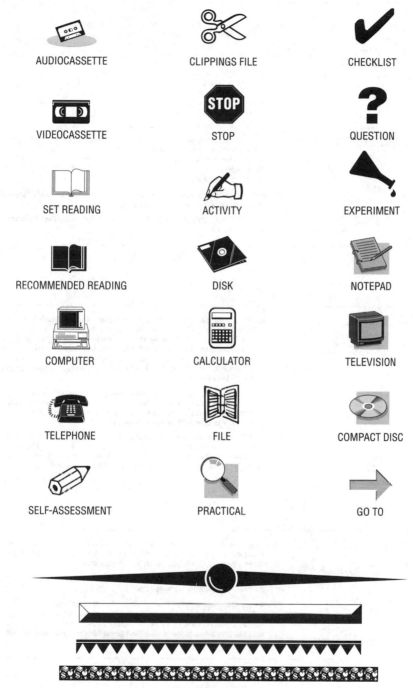

AUDIOCASSETTE

CLIPPINGS FILE

CHECKLIST

VIDEOCASSETTE

STOP

QUESTION

SET READING

ACTIVITY

EXPERIMENT

RECOMMENDED READING

DISK

NOTEPAD

COMPUTER

CALCULATOR

TELEVISION

TELEPHONE

FILE

COMPACT DISC

SELF-ASSESSMENT

PRACTICAL

GO TO

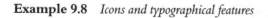

STUDENT STOPPERS

Example 9.8   *Icons and typographical features*

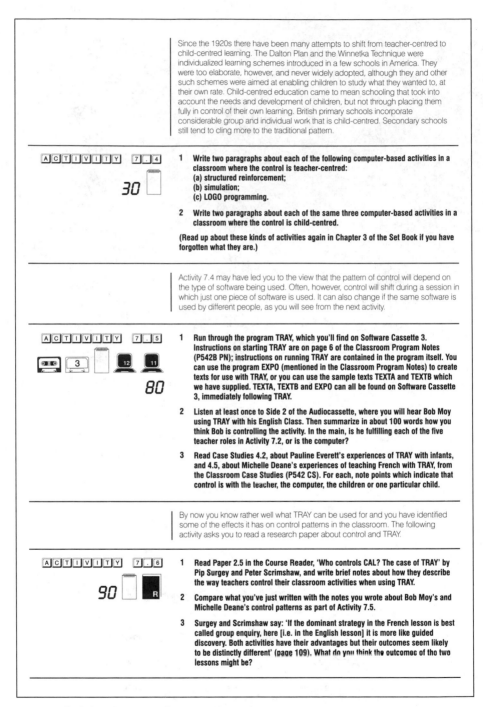

Since the 1920s there have been many attempts to shift from teacher-centred to child-centred learning. The Dalton Plan and the Winnetka Technique were individualized learning schemes introduced in a few schools in America. They were too elaborate, however, and never widely adopted, although they and other such schemes were aimed at enabling children to study what they wanted to, at their own rate. Child-centred education came to mean schooling that took into account the needs and development of children, but not through placing them fully in control of their own learning. British primary schools incorporate considerable group and individual work that is child-centred. Secondary schools still tend to cling more to the traditional pattern.

ACTIVITY 7.4

30

1   Write two paragraphs about each of the following computer-based activities in a classroom where the control is teacher-centred:
(a) structured reinforcement;
(b) simulation;
(c) LOGO programming.

2   Write two paragraphs about each of the same three computer-based activities in a classroom where the control is child-centred.

(Read up about these kinds of activities again in Chapter 3 of the Set Book if you have forgotten what they are.)

Activity 7.4 may have led you to the view that the pattern of control will depend on the type of software being used. Often, however, control will shift during a session in which just one piece of software is used. It can also change if the same software is used by different people, as you will see from the next activity.

ACTIVITY 7.5

80

1   Run through the program TRAY, which you'll find on Software Cassette 3. Instructions on starting TRAY are on page 6 of the Classroom Program Notes (P542B PN); instructions on running TRAY are contained in the program itself. You can use the program EXPO (mentioned in the Classroom Program Notes) to create texts for use with TRAY, or you can use the sample texts TEXTA and TEXTB which we have supplied. TEXTA, TEXTB and EXPO can all be found on Software Cassette 3, immediately following TRAY.

2   Listen at least once to Side 2 of the Audiocassette, where you will hear Bob Moy using TRAY with his English Class. Then summarize in about 100 words how you think Bob is controlling the activity. In the main, is he fulfilling each of the five teacher roles in Activity 7.2, or is the computer?

3   Read Case Studies 4.2, about Pauline Everett's experiences of TRAY with infants, and 4.5, about Michelle Deane's experiences of teaching French with TRAY, from the Classroom Case Studies (P542 CS). For each, note points which indicate that control is with the teacher, the computer, the children or one particular child.

By now you know rather well what TRAY can be used for and you have identified some of the effects it has on control patterns in the classroom. The following activity asks you to read a research paper about control and TRAY.

ACTIVITY 7.6

90

1   Read Paper 2.5 in the Course Reader, 'Who controls CAL? The case of TRAY' by Pip Surgey and Peter Scrimshaw, and write brief notes about how they describe the way teachers control their classroom activities when using TRAY.

2   Compare what you've just written with the notes you wrote about Bob Moy's and Michelle Deane's control patterns as part of Activity 7.5.

3   Surgey and Scrimshaw say: 'If the dominant strategy in the French lesson is best called group enquiry, here [i.e. in the English lesson] it is more like guided discovery. Both activities have their advantages but their outcomes seem likely to be distinctly different' (page 109). What do you think the outcomes of the two lessons might be?

Example 9.9   *Over-use of icons*

9.3.2 Layout and design

There is no shortage of variations in the layout and design of teaching material and ways to identify activities. The layout for multiple choice questions of the yes/no, true/false, or selecting one or more from four or more alternative types will be different from those demanding calculations or a written/drawn response. The activities can be identified by a different font, font size or colour, they can be indented, placed in a box, flagged by halftone shading and combined with icons and other typographical devices.

However, whatever is chosen the layout and design adopted will create a *house style* – a style that must be consistent through the learning material. It should be possible simply to scan the screens of a CD-ROM or study guide and recognize the activities immediately – as well as the constituents of them. Problems emerge when there is no consistency and when it simply isn't clear whether an activity or a rhetorical question has been posed.

9.3.3 Space and time allocations

A decision about the space to allocate to an activity will depend upon the teaching or training medium you are using. Computer-based and CD-ROM training materials usually have a facility that allows learners to type in their response or insert entries into a database so that comments can be forwarded or subsequent analyses completed – with the space expanding to accept whatever is written. If a printed study guide is used a decision to leave a space for a response or to save paper by including a phrase like 'Write your answer to the question in your notebook' can be adopted. However, with regard to printed self-instructional material the evidence is clear; if you fail to provide space for learners to respond to the activity the chances are that they will not respond to it. The more space you provide, the more learners will write. Furthermore, if you provide a series of headings, a grid, a matrix or the axes for a graph, learners will use the framework provided and respond to the activity (Lockwood, 1992). Example 9.10 illustrates an activity requiring a calculator and which provides a grid for the response. Contrary to the claim that leaving space for a response is a waste of paper, it does fulfil a valuable teaching role and prompts a response.

9.4 How do you think activities are used by learners?

You are likely to get a broad range of responses to Question 4. Some will maintain that learners must do the activities because subsequent material builds on the answers – they cannot proceed unless they have done them! Others may say that they suspect learners will not bother doing them but will simply read the question and turn immediately to the feedback. A few are likely to remark that they simply do not know. You may even have someone who asks whether there is any evidence indicating what learners do.

TRY SOME YOURSELF

3(i) Complete the table of values below and so draw the graphs of:

(a) $y = 2x^2$ (b) $y = 2x^2 + 1$

x	-2.5	-2	-1.5	-1	-0.5	0	0.5	1	1.5	2	2.5
$y = 2x^2$											
$y = 2x^2 + 1$											

(ii) Complete a similar table of values and so draw the graphs of:

(a) $y = 0.5x^2$ (b) $y = 0.5x^2 + 1$

(iii) Complete a similar table of values and so draw the graphs of:

(a) $y = -2x^2$ (b) $y = -2x^2 + 1$

This exercise shows that there is no quick method for plotting a quadratic. Your graph will be more accurate if you plot lots of points. It's always a good idea to plot several points around the bottom of the parabola (or top if it's upside down) to get a better shape. Of course the accuracy also depends upon the scales that you choose, so if you need a particularly accurate graph use large scales.

You should be able to draw both graphs on the same axes.

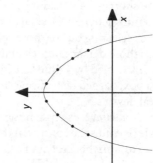

Example 9.10 *Activity identifying the use of a calculator and providing a grid for the response*

Compelling evidence (Lockwood, 1992) indicates that learners typically operate within a 'Cost–Benefit Analysis model'. It sounds very grand, but basically learners constantly balance the perceived benefits that activities offer with the costs they will incur in responding to them; it is a dynamic process (Figure 9.3). There appear to be three main benefits: course-focused benefits; self-focused benefits; and assignment-focused benefits.

Benefits
- Course-focused
- Self-focused
- Assignment-focused

Costs
- Consumed study time
- Degradation
- Deference
- Guilt and inadequacy

Figure 9.3 *Elements within the cost–benefit analysis model*

Course-focused benefits are those that relate to learning from a course or topic: the concepts, ideas and arguments under discussion, and the techniques, procedures or skills being practised. For learners in this category, the activities are perceived as contributing to their understanding of the material. A typical comment from a learner would be:

> If it looks like it is going to tie in and it is going to increase my understanding later in the course... then I will work through it very, very methodically.

Self-focused benefits are those that relate to one's learning and development as a person: the opportunities they provide for ideas and arguments to be explored or re-considered, previous assumptions to be challenged and personal interest to be awakened, developed or extended. For learners in this category the activities

> ...are just trying to make you take a wider stance and... think more openly about it and to question your own thinking and to probe your thinking and probe your own viewpoint.

Assignment-focused benefits are those that contribute directly to answering a test or some other form of assignment and that provide an opportunity either to think about the issues to be discussed or to provide materials to be used in it. Learners in this category often remark:

> if it's relevant to the [assignment] and if I feel I can use it, I would definitely do it... and do it properly.... I won't do anything unless it's totally relevant to getting a good grade.

The benefits from activities are balanced by the costs – the major one being the study time they consume. There is often a limited amount of time available, and such time spent on activities means that there is less for other parts of the course. A typical comment from a student would be:

> I rarely go anywhere near the time that you are supposed to spend on [activities]... you are under too much pressure to do that.

Learners incur other intellectual and emotional costs as a result of their decision not to complete activities or not to respond to them as fully as they feel is desirable. Learners *degrade* activities, show undue *deference* to the comments of the author and often feel *guilty and inadequate* as learners. In contrast to learners who complete activities along the lines suggested, many reduce the intellectual demands or *degrade* them; thus making it simpler than intended and less time-consuming than expected. Often the demands are recognized by the learner but substituted for less taxing ones. The following comment is typical:

> [The activity] asked you to compare the different views and assess the strengths and weaknesses of the two... I didn't bother... I just read them and decided which one was closest to my own view.

In contrast to learners who have confidence in the arguments they marshal, or answers which are different from those of the author but equally valid, there are others who, upon discovering that their response is not the same as that provided in the feedback, abandon their own and adopt the writer's without exploring the value of the activity, without attempting to resolve the differences of opinion or confirm the validity of their answer. In such circumstances learners can be said to show undue *deference* to the comments of the author. The following comment is representative:

> If [my own answer] differs I usually choose the author's and change mine to suit... I usually end up taking the author's answer in place of my own... when it comes to revision I would not remember what was right and what was wrong.

In contrast to those students who regard themselves as effective and efficient learners, who regard the activities as a resource and who respond to some of them and not others as they judge necessary, there are others who incur an emotional cost in not completing them. These learners, who fail to complete the activities along the lines suggested, regard themselves as inadequate and feel guilty. They feel they are not doing themselves justice in their study, not getting from the course all they could. Such learners frequently make comments like:

> The activity aids your understanding, it certainly does... and I'm a fool to myself for not doing them... I'd taken the lazy way out and not done it... I'm not taking advantage of these activities.

A much fuller discussion of the benefits and costs that learners perceive is provided elsewhere (Lockwood, 1992).

9.4.1 How can you influence learner use?

Teachers and trainers who are assembling self-instructional material need to realize that they have little control over the way their students study. Learners, even school-age learners, are likely to have domestic, work and social demands that compete with study demands. For many it will be arranging their study around their life – *not* their life around their study!

Classic educational studies have indicated that learners are directly influenced, even dominated, by assessment demands (see Miller and Parlett 1974). In a replication of this study (Lockwood, 1992), a substantial proportion of learners were found to be 'TMA Dominated'; they geared their entire study to answering the TMA (Tutor Marked Assignment). Anything that wasn't directly relevant to answering the assessment questions was ignored; their study was dominated by assignment demands. Other classic studies have indicated that learners' Orientation to Study and their Approach to Study (Morgan, 1993) have a major influence upon their study. As a consequence, it would be prudent to regard activities as a resource (along with all the other course components) that is offered to learners. However, in doing so it is important that you identify the benefits that activities offer as well as the costs that learners will incur in responding to them.

If you believe that the reasons that emerged from your consideration of Question 1 (Why do we need activities in our self-instructional teaching material?) are valid, the following features are likely to encourage students to respond to them (see Figure 9.4).

- Context
- Title
- Rationale
- Icon/house style
- Time allocation
- Instructions
- Example
- Response space, grid or framework
- Feedback

Figure 9.4 *Key constituents of an activity*

- *Context*
  The activity should emerge logically from the context of the teaching material; it should represent valid questions to ask and tasks to undertake – objectives to realize.
- *Title*
  Each activity should have a clear and concise title that encapsulates the nature of the proposed task. It not only orientates the learner, but is useful in referring to the task in any communication with you.

- *Rationale*
  A rationale provides an indication of why it is worth the time and effort to respond to the activity; it is vital. If you cannot think of a good reason why it is
  worth posing the activity, perhaps it isn't worth posing at all! Trivial activities get
  the treatment they deserve from learners; they are skipped. Unfortunately, the
  effect is that often subsequent activities, which may be worthwhile, receive the
  same cursory treatment.

- *Icon/house style*
  An icon or typographical representation should flag the presence of the activity
  and contribute to the overall house style adopted. It would be worthwhile explaining what this icon represents in an Introduction and Guide to the course.

- *Time allocation*
  Learners will come to your course with different abilities, interests, backgrounds
  and skills. As such, it is extremely difficult to know how long they will take responding to the activity. However, by drawing upon your previous experience
  you can estimate a time allocation which you feel that learners are likely to
  spend. If you are able to run a field trial or developmentally test your material
  you will be able to assemble evidence indicating what learners can do in the time
  they spend on the activity. Of course, even this will provide a range of times from
  which you need to adopt the optimum. This not only gives an indication of the
  scope and depth of the answers, but also provides material to use in your feedback to learners.
      A typical fault is to underestimate the time students will need to spend on ac-
  tivities, which will cause them to fall behind in their study and eventually discard
  activities to 'save time'.

- *Instructions*
  The instructions for the activity must be clear and precise. You will not be
  around to witness the puzzled expressions or to respond to the requests for clarification. The best way to ensure this is to try out the activities in a developmental
  testing exercise before you finalize the material.

- *Example*
  An example of the answer(s) you are expecting, perhaps within an illustration of
  possible guidelines or under a range of conditions, can reinforce your instructions and guide the learner. Sometimes examples of plausible but inappropriate
  solutions or typical errors and pitfalls can be valuable. No self-instruction golf
  video would be complete without an illustration of the effects of typical faults
  and how to correct them.

- *Response space, grid or framework*
  Provide an appropriate series of headings, subheadings, grids, frameworks or
  spaces for a response – all the evidence shows that it will encourage learners.

- *Feedback*
  Provide feedback that is commensurate with the task you have posed the learners – using the framework you originally provided. Of course, there may not be
  an answer. You may only be able to provide alternatives, a commentary or discussion of the possible reactions. You also need to provide this feedback as close

as possible to the point where the activity was posed. If you really want to annoy learners, put the feedback in appendices, at the end of the module or in another computer file. To avoid the student inadvertently seeing the answer, or commentary, it can simply be rolled over to the next page or the next computer screen.

If your activities embody these features there is every likelihood of them being successful – and satisfying the reasons you listed for including them in Question 1.

References

Central Planning Unit (1991) *The Road Traffic Act, 1991: An Officers' Guide*, Central Planning Unit, Harrogate.

Evans, T (1989) Fiddling while the tome turns: reflections of a distance education development consultant, in *Development, Design and Distance Education* (ed M Parer), Centre for Distance Learning, Gippsland Institute of Advanced Education, Churchill, Victoria.

Farrally, M (1991) *An Introduction to the Structure of the Body*, The National Coaching Foundation, Leeds, in conjunction with The Scottish Sports Council, Edinburgh.

Lockwood, F (1992) *Activities in Self-Instructional Texts*, Kogan Page, London.

Miller, C M L and Parlett, M (1974) *Up to the Mark. A study of the examination game*, Society for Research in Higher Education, Monograph 21.

Morgan, A (1993) *Improving your students' learning*, Kogan Page, London.

NACT (1990) *NACT Training Package*, National Association of Clinical Tutors, London.

Nation, D (1991) Teaching texts and independent learning, in *Beyond the Text: Contemporary Writing on Distance Education* (eds Evans, T and King, B), Deakin University Press, Geelong.

Nunan, T (1991) *An Introduction to Research Paradigms in Distance Education*, Deakin University Press, Geelong.

Open University (1987) *EH 221 Educational Computing*, The Open University Press, Milton Keynes.

Ostwald, M S and Chen, S E (1993) Implementing problem-based learning in distance education, *Media and Technology for Human Resource Development*, 6(1), 25–32.

Rothkopf, E Z (1970) The concept of mathemagenic activities, *Review of Educational Research*, 40(3), 325–35.

Rowntree, D (1974) *Educational Technology in Curriculum Development*, Harper & Row, London.

Rowntree, D (1990) *Teaching Through Self-Instruction*, Kogan Page, London.

Rowntree, D (1992) *Exploring Open and Distance Learning*, Kogan Page, London.

Sanders, N M (1966) *Classroom Questions*, Harper & Row, New York.

Science Museum (1991) *Flight Lab*, London, Science Museum.

Thunhurst, A (1990) *Front of House Operations*, Macmillian Education, London.

Chapter 10

Learner workload and readability

Many teachers and trainers develop confidence in equating the volume of teaching material, mix of different media, the constituent tasks and their relative difficulty with realistic estimates of study time; time that equates to the workload associated with the particular course of study. How do they do that? How can you ensure that your material is on target in terms of study time and pitched at the appropriate level? The following questions should help you consider some of the key issues.

1. Why is learner workload important?
    (Consider the implications for under- and over-length material.)

2. How much time do your learners have for study?
    (Consider formal statements of the study time expected.)

3. How can we estimate the level of difficulty of prose material?
    (Consider any existing methods or indices.)

4. How have others calculated learner study time?
    (Consider existing practical or theoretical guidelines available.)

5. How could you estimate learner study time?
    (Consider any 'Rules of Thumb' or computer programmes available.)

10.1 Why is learner workload important?

In recent years there has been a significant change in the way learners are regarded. It has changed from 'students will take what we give them' to 'clients who not only need to be attracted to a course but satisfied with the teaching or training provided' (see Figure 10.1). At the same time, there has been increasing attention to quality assurance indicators with government, industry and commerce monitoring performance. You will be aware of the increasingly competitive teaching and training environment within which we are working – an environment that spans local regions and states, countries and continents. Today you can select from any one of 33,000 open and distance learning courses in further and higher education, available from over 100 countries and almost 1000 institutions – providing you satisfy the entry requirements and can afford it (International Centre for Distance Learning, 1998). Learners are no longer restricted to the local teaching or training provider. Furthermore, just like high street consumers, learners are becoming increasingly aware of their rights and are becoming more discerning. In this context two things typically dominate the lives of learners – the course assessment demands and the time available for study – learner workload. In terms of workload the usual cry is that there is too much work to do in the time – not the reverse. However, if clients are paying for a product you can be assured that they will demand value for money. The provision of inadequate, superficial and under-length material will be criticized just as much as daunting and over-length material.

It is fairly common for teachers and trainers to say they are working too hard. It is also fairly common to discover that they are expecting learners to work too hard – and it is counter-productive. More is not better! This is especially true in those institutions that are offering self-instructional material and are making the transition from a private form of teaching (within the confines of the classroom, workshop, laboratory or clinical setting) to a public forum – where anyone can see and judge the quality and quantity of the material provided. It is so tempting to elaborate that explanation, provide that example, include another exercise, to make the teaching as detailed and comprehensive as possible; especially when one knows that colleagues around the world will have access to this material in the near future. (For those who believe that the self-instructional materials they are assembling are for the eyes of their own students, I suggest they think again. I'm aware of several teachers and trainers who have registered as students merely to get their hands on course material!)

Generating over-length material is counter-productive, especially for learners who may not have your reading and study skills (Macdonald-Ross and Scott, 1995a, page 2):

- Change from students to clients
- Increasingly competitive teaching/learning environment
- More discerning learners – expect what they pay for
- Monitoring of quality assurance indicators
- Learning often dominated by course assessment demands and time available for study
- Self-instructional material typically over-length – effect is counter-productive
- Effect of transition from private to public teaching
- Over-length material makes excessive demands on everyone – not just teachers and learners
- Teaching and training must be cost-effective – provided to an agreed budget

Figure 10.1 *Why is learner workload important?*

It has been shown by Klare in a series of studies that the effect of a mismatch between reading skill and text readability is more pronounced if subjects are put under time pressure.

Over-length material makes excessive demands on everyone associated with it – from the authors who write it, secretaries who type and assemble it, and editors and graphic designers who put it into the house style, to printers or software specialists who put it into the required format, etc. Furthermore, all of this costs money. Those courses that are not cost-effective have a bleak future in today's economic climate.

10.2 How much time do your students have for study?

The comments in Chapter 5, under the heading 'How much time will they have available for study in a typical week?' are relevant here (see page 60); they are summarized, together with the comments below, in Figure 10.2.

If you are unsure how much time your learners have for study, you can always ask them. If they are following a course you can ask them how much time they are devoting to it and determine whether they are spending the amount of time they expected, and use this data both to monitor workload and to guide future courses. Is this a practice your institution follows? The Student Research Centre, within the Open University Institute of Educational Technology, collects such data each year from all new courses and has built up a profile of learner workload over a number of years. Evidence from recent surveys of new courses indicates that the average study times within the Faculties of Arts, Science, Social Science, Mathematics and Technology, and the School of Education, Centre for Modern Languages and OU Business School were 11 hours, 11 hours, 12 hours, 9.5 hours, 10.5 hours, 9.5 hours, 10 hours and 9.5 hours, respectively (Open University, 1997a–h).

- Specification of study time as part of course validation/accreditation procedures
- OU expects 12–14 hours/week study for 32 weeks for 6 years to gain a degree (without credit exemptions)
- Impact of personal, work, domestic and leisure commitments on study time available
- Cumulative effect on workload if part(s) over-length
- Problems in sustaining effort over months and years
- Evidence that full-time students are prepared to commit about 40 hours/week on study
- Need to investigate and monitor learner workloads and effect on course performance/dropout

Figure 10.2 *Time available for study*

The first impression is one of consistency in terms of the average study time – when the target is 10–14 hours per week. However, the reports state that 'Students who claimed to have studied over 40 hours a week have been excluded from the analysis'. The effect, of course, is to reduce the average figures considerably. There is also evidence, although now some 15 years old (Woodley and Parlett, 1983), that over-length material is a major reason for students dropping out of courses. If students have 'dropped out' they are unlikely to return end-of-course questionnaires which are likely to indicate excessive workloads, which again is likely to distort the above figures. Finally, there is some evidence (Chambers, 1994) that when students are asked to indicate the amount of time they spend studying they systematically underestimate it! One suggested explanation is that learners are likely to be reluctant to identify themselves as 'slow learners' (compared with the study times published in course materials) and modify their answers accordingly! Thus the average study times indicated may be misleading. Needless to say, you will need to collect your own data and interpret it according.

10.3 How can we estimate the level of difficulty of teaching material – of prose material?

There is more to teaching material than just text. The audio and video sequences that may form part of the teaching are likely to be important, maybe even vital, parts of the package. Diagrams, maps, charts, figures, tables, practical tasks and computer-based exercises are also likely to be integral parts of the teaching material – otherwise why include them? It is therefore limiting to consider only the textual components in terms of their difficulty and implications for learner workload. However, it is likely that textual material will constitute a major part of the teaching material – be it in the form of instructions, case studies, articles, technical reports or textbooks. Furthermore, sources are available that provide advice on teaching components, ranging from project work (Henry, 1994) to diagrams (Lowe, 1993).

You could, of course, merely trust your own judgement as to the relative difficulty of material, a judgement that may be based upon years of experience. If you do not have such experience, or want to consider an alternative, you might like to consider two methods of estimating the readability of material: the Cloze Test and the Fog Index.

10.3.1 Cloze Test

The Cloze Test is extremely simple. It is based upon samples of the textual material from which a series of words have been omitted, and the test is to write in the missing words. The introduction from the IET Survey of Reading skills (Scott and Macdonald-Ross, 1995, page 9) illustrates this readily.

Only one word has _____ left out each time _____ this is indicated by a continuous line. All the lines _____ of equal length, so they _____ no clue as to the _____ of the missing word. Spelling is _____ important, as long as it _____ clear what the word _____ that you intended to _____ in the gap. If at _____ you can't think of a _____ to put in the gap, read on and _____ back to it later. You may also go back and change your choices.

Cloze Tests do vary somewhat but typically delete every fifth or seventh word. The words written in by the subject are compared with a short list of acceptable words. The Cloze Test is not only extremely simple to conduct and score but has demonstrated that it is extremely valid and reliable at predicting the readability of prose material. It measures what it is designed to measure and does so consistently. It is because of this that colleagues within the OU (Scott and Macdonald-Ross, 1995) administered three short Cloze Tests to approximately 3,000 students as part of their postal survey of OU students' reading skills. The sample included students from all five foundation courses and four levels of educational qualification.

Passage One was drawn from a basic skills screening test – an indicator of basic functional literacy. Passage Two was typical of OU Foundation course material – it equated to the editorial one would expect in a broadsheet newspaper. Passage Three was an extract from a book review in the *Times Higher Educational Supplement* and typical of the text one would expect to encounter in academic study. In interpreting test scoring it is argued that those with a test score of 60 per cent or better can satisfactorily comprehend the material. A score of between 40 per cent and 60 per cent indicates partial comprehension, and less than 40 per cent indicates inadequate comprehension.

Almost all students achieved a score of 60 per cent or better on Passage One; they were virtually all functionally literate. On Passage Two almost one-third scored less than 60 per cent, indicating that they demonstrated only partial comprehension. However, on Passage Three almost one-third scored less than 40 per cent

– indicating inadequate comprehension – and two-thirds scored between 40 per cent and 60 per cent, indicating only partial comprehension. In all, about 95 per cent of the students had difficulty in comprehending the passage!

For an institution that prides itself on the quality of its teaching, and pitching the material at an appropriate level, the findings were sobering. The authors remark (Macdonald-Ross and Scott, 1995a):

> ...most entering students enrolled for OU foundation courses have reading skills which are not at the appropriate level for working with academic prose, and many are seriously deficient.

If the OU, with over 25 years' experience of producing self-instructional material, can produce teaching material that one-third of new students finds unintelligible (partial comprehension), perhaps it would be prudent to check the difficulty of your material.

10.3.2 Fog Index

In Figure 10.3 you will see two paragraphs, each of 100 words. Read through both paragraphs and decide which paragraph is most difficult and why. What is it about one of the two paragraphs that makes it more difficult to study – and as a result will probably take longer to study?

A major problem facing both the writer of distance teaching material and students is workload. In conventional teaching it is possible to continually assess the comprehension of students and adjust the speed and complexity of the teaching. It is possible to finish a session early or return to it next week. In distance teaching the problem is to assemble a package of material that can be studied by the majority of students in the time allocated. Over-length material takes longer to write. It takes longer to type, edit and print. It takes longer to study – if students study it!

A third type of ethical dilemma arises in deciding on whether to deceive participants, even if it will be only temporary. Some researchers react to this dilemma by arguing for an absolute code of ethics, which would forbid any researcher to use certain practices under any circumstances; others would leave such decisions to the conscience of the individual researcher concerned. These decisions are complex since they ultimately involve a judgement as to the practical value of the research project. In paragraphs below I illustrate *trade offs* that often occur between ethical and other commitments, in making a particular research decision.

Figure 10.3 *Factors influencing the readability of textual material*

There are no prizes for identifying the bottom paragraph as likely to be more diffi-cult – but why? It is likely that if you presented the two paragraphs in Figure 10.3 to a group of colleagues they would say that the bottom paragraph has longer words and longer sentences. You may get other suggestions, such as that the bottom one is more abstract, but the two things you can definitely measure, and measure easily, are the lengths of words and sentences. In fact, these two indicators of the readability of prose material have been used repeated to devise measures of difficulty. They were used in a formula to calculate the Fog Index (Gunning, 1968); according to Gunning, the two things that made a text difficult to read, or foggy, was the number of words of three or more syllables and long sentences. The formula that Gunning created, and which is used to calculate a Fog Index, is given below:

Fog Index = (Average number of words per sentence + Percentage of words with three or more syllables) × 0.4

There are 100 words in each of the two paragraphs in Figure 10.3. The top one con-sists of seven sentences, the bottom one of four sentences. The average numbers of words per sentence in the two paragraphs are thus 14.3 and 25 respectively.

In the top paragraph there are 11 words of three or more syllables (the percentage is therefore 11), and in the bottom paragraph there are 25 words; a percentage of 25. If these data are inserted into the formula (see below), the Fog Indices for the two paragraphs are 10.12 and 20.00 respectively.

Fog Index (top paragraph) = (14.3 + 11) × 0.4 = 10.12
Fog Index (bottom paragraph) = (25.0 + 25) × 0.4 = 20.00

Gunning spent years investigating the readability of textual material in a whole range of academic and technical areas and with a broad age range of learners.

You may find it useful to discover the Fog Index of the materials you present your learners and check what others believe should be the typical index range of appro-priately pitched material. However, you do not have to do this mechanically, as I did in the above example. Computer software is now available that will assemble differ-ent indices and will do this automatically. For example, a facility is available when using the Grammar tool in Microsoft Word that will allow you to calculate an index of readability called the Flesch Reading Ease Score. This is a widely used index and has been demonstrated to be extremely reliable and valid at predicting the difficulty of prose material (Klare, 1984). When Flesch Reading Ease Scores were calculated for the two paragraphs in Figure 10.3 the following indicators were available in sec-onds:

	First paragraph	Second paragraph
Counts		
Words	100	100
Characters	483	543
Paragraphs	1	1
Sentences	7	4

Averages

Sentences per paragraph	7	4
Words per sentence	14.29	25.00
Characters per word	4.74	5.35
Readability		
Passive sentences	14.29	00.00
Flesch Reading Ease	52.75	32.56

The indicators confirm there are 100 words in each paragraph, that the first paragraph has seven sentences and the second paragraph has four; that the average numbers of words per sentence are 14.29 and 25 respectively. The calculation of the Flesch Reading Ease Score is based on the average number of syllables per word and the average number of words per sentence with scores ranging from 0 to 100. It is suggested that standard writing averages should be between 60 and 70, with a high score indicating the greater number of people who can readily understand the text. In the case of the two paragraphs the scores are 52.75 and 32.56, and the second paragraph is considered significantly more difficult than the first. While I suspect that this is fairly obvious from your reading of the two paragraphs, the computer software would allow you to check whole modules or even courses.

Other software packages are available that will provide similar indices – average sentence length, words not in the program vocabulary, words used repeatedly, etc. The beauty of such software is that you can make simple modifications to successive drafts (shortening sentence length, substituting more common words, deleting repetitive words and phrases) and see immediately the effect upon the series of indicators. Field trials suggest that such simple modifications significantly reduce the difficulty of the material.

10.4 How have others calculated student study time?

Different institutions have adopted different practices in trying to equate the collection of learning materials that represent a course with the study time it is likely to consume. The three most common approaches have been based on:

- notional hours per week (in the range 12–14 hours per week)
- page numbers per week (typically 48–56 pages per week)
- words per unit (in the range 15,000–18,000 words per week).

10.4.1 Hours available for study per week

Contributors to the Hale Report (see 'How much time will they have available for study in a typical week' page 60) were extremely thorough in noting all of the components of a course that consume study time and which would ultimately contribute to the degree. The data they provided enabled universities to compare their demands and helped those planning the OU to ensure parity, in terms of workload, with other UK universities. The OU equated a degree, in workload terms, to about 2,500 hours of study time or 12–14 hours per week for 32 weeks over a period of 6 years.

Many institutions, in recent years, have indicated similar notional time allocations. However, a problem emerges when these notional time allocations bear little or no resemblance to actual study time or when significant study components are omitted. For example, a course offered by the University of the South Pacific, which indicated that students could expect to spend 'six hours per week for the semester', suffered a massive dropout rate in the first half-semester; the course lost 85 per cent of its students. An investigation revealed (Lockwood *et al.*, 1988) that the course was grossly over-length, with estimated study times of 20+ hours and 30+ hours per week rather than the 6 hours that were estimated! The effect on students was devastating.

Where the teaching or training on a course is shared between a number of staff members there is always the temptation to assume that a particularly heavy week, in terms of workload, will be balanced by a subsequent lighter week. Of course, if all the weeks of study migrate to the heavy end of the scale the effect is cumulative – and problematic for all concerned.

Within the OU it is common practice to include a notional time for course assessment within the overall estimated study time. However, those assembling the report noted that while courses typically allocated '...about a couple of hours per week', those responsible admitted that this was often exceeded! Furthermore, it is not uncommon for teachers and trainers, or whole institutions, to regard time spent on course assignments to be *on top* of the course!

10.4.2 Use of page numbers to estimate student workload

There are apparent advantages to restricting authors to a set number of pages, say 48 pages, and equating this to one week of student study time. The physical size of the study guides or associated printed materials would be consistent. Further estimates of the ratios of text, photographs, diagrams, charts, etc. may allow secretaries, designers and editors to plan their work more accurately. It would be possible to refine estimates of print, storage and postal costs, etc. (However, the growth in online courses, teaching via the WWW and provision of material on CD-ROM will not only influence these estimates but increasingly make them inappropriate.)

Unfortunately the conceptual complexity of the teaching material makes equating simple page lengths to study time extremely suspect. Depending on the font and page size it is possible to present different amounts of textual material. For example, a single-column A4 page may contain about 800 words; an A5 page (half the size of A4) might contain only 300 words in the same type size and style, since the page margins will take up proportionately more space on the A5 page than on the A4 page. It may be possible for the average student (one in the nodal group) to study a text of, say, 48 pages in 12 hours; however, a text of the same length – but more conceptually dense, perhaps containing exercises, activities, etc. could take a student

112 hours! This is not a crude exaggeration. When the Open University Preparatory materials were evaluated (Lockwood, 1989) one student reported completing a 'study' of 70+ pages in under 20 minutes; another student, studying the same material, reported a study time of 180 hours! (Many parts of the Preparatory materials were associated with mini pre-tests – if students completed the pre-test satisfactorily they could skip the subsequent material. If they didn't perform well on the pre-test they were advised to work through subsequent material systematically.)

10.4.3 Word length of the teaching material

Word processing packages can readily give estimates of the word length of textual material, irrespective of page and font size. However, the problem of assessing the level of difficulty remains. Computer packages are available that will allow you to assess the readability of your textual material, calculating Fog Indices and Flesch Reading Ease Scores. These and other programmes, typically based on the average length of sentences and words of three or more syllables, do offer a reliable way of determining a readability score – a measure of syntactic and semantic complexity that predicts difficulty in text. The problem comes in equating these levels of complexity to student workload. This was evident in a recent Technical Report (Macdonald-Ross and Scott, 1995b) that revealed large variations in readability between topics, between courses and between authors. It also revealed significant differences in the word totals for Open University Foundation courses; for example, 1,175,000 words for the Arts Foundation course A102 compared with 642,500 for the Technology Foundation course T102. Study of these two courses was expected to consume similar amounts of study time; they were identical in terms of their credit rating towards a degree.

A further problem arises when trying to estimate the study time for non-textual components. The study of a map, chart, diagram, photograph, drawing or whatever could involve a student in anything from a few seconds' observation to hours of work. Maybe you have spent merely seconds viewing a painting and at other times considerably longer; you may have glanced at a diagram or spent hours working through it. Equating page length or word length to study time is not easy. Similarly, electronically based activities (self-assessment questions, in-text questions, exercises, and CBT and CAL packages, as well as computer-mediated communication) could involve a few moments' reflection or hours of work. Indeed, many teachers note the emphasis they give to requiring students to think, reflect or practise particular skills. The study time associated with these components bears no relationship to the number of words or pages associated with them.

10.5 How could you estimate student study time?

One solution to the problem of determining the readability of the textual material and estimating student study time would be to ask authors to specify, at each draft stage, and at *handover*, the components that contribute to the teaching package, to calculate the Flesch Reading Ease Score or Fog Index and to estimate the student study time for each of them. This need not be a mechanical process, but could allow them to use, and justify, their estimates. However, how does one equate the difficulty of teaching material with student study time?

Students come to the teaching material with a variety of motives, expectations, interests, skills, abilities and previous experience. Such a heterogeneous group will obviously study different course components in different ways – consuming different amounts of time. What some see as essential others will view as optional. What is new to some students, and which will require an input of study time, will be familiar to others and be skimmed over. Any estimate can, at best, cater for the majority for whom the material is new.

One solution is to employ a simple rule of thumb based on material being 'easy', of 'moderate' difficulty or 'difficult' for a majority of the students and to equate this with a corresponding study time allocation. Teaching material judged to be 'easy' (for the target audience and at this point in the course) is estimated at 100 words per minute (w/m) to study. Material judged of 'moderate difficulty' (again, for a particular audience and point in the course) is estimated at 70 w/m and 'difficult' material at 40 w/m. Note that these estimates relate to study times, not reading speeds. We are all aware that it is possible to read printed material at 200 w/m, 300 w/m or more. However, in the context of teaching material we are interested in study times.

Example 10.1 illustrates the constituents of a typical module of a self-instructional course – textual material, activities, non-text media, face-to-face teaching, electronic media and assessment material. The study time likely to be associated with the textual material can be estimated by use of the above rule of thumb. It would be possible to draw upon your previous experience and estimate the time it would take a typical learner to complete each of the activities and, depending on their purpose, the non-text media. These study times, or rather the range of times, could be confirmed in a developmental testing exercise or field trial. The time allocated to any face-to-face teaching (tutorial, day schools, etc.) could be estimated with time allocated before, during and after the actual face-to-face contact. Somewhat more difficult would be the task of estimating the essential on-line time associated with the electronic media used on any course. Evidence from research at the OU (Mason, 1994) suggests that computer-based activities can become addictive and consume enormous amounts of study time. Finally, the time allocated for assignments and other assessment material can be estimated – with the realization that many students spend a disproportionate amount of time on assignments.

An illustration of how these estimates can be combined is provided in Example 10.2. While it is acknowledged that each of the estimates is based on subjective judgements, and there is a danger of errors being compounded, in practice it has proved to be remarkably accurate and resilient across many faculties and at different levels within the OU and elsewhere over the last 15 years.

Textual material	**Method of calculation**
Study guide, set books, articles, extracts and other textual materials	Simple rule of thumb, based on 'easy' (100 words per minute), 'moderate' (70 words per minute), 'difficult' (40 words per minute)
Activities in texts	
Self-assessment questions, exercises, in-text questions, experiments, reflection and practice, and other activities	Estimate of study time during which the majority (three-quarters to two-thirds) of students could complete it satisfactorily
Non-text media	
Photos, maps, charts, diagrams and other non-text media	Depending on the purpose of studying the image – estimate the likely study time
Face-to-face	
Tutorial(s), field trips, day schools, residential schools and other face-to-face sessions	Estimated study time – before, during and after the sessions
Electronic media	
Computer-mediated communication, email, computer-based training, computer-assisted learning, CD-ROM activities and other electronic media	Estimates of essential online time
Assessment material	
Tutor-marked assignments, computer-marked assignments, project work, examination(s) and other assessment activities	Estimates of time associated with these tasks

Example 10.1   *A framework within which to estimate student workload*

There is a simple way to demonstrate your ability to assess the relative difficulty of material and estimate learner workload. You can select one of your own teaching modules, identify the constituent parts, note the difficulty you feel they will cause your learners and estimate the study time for the constituent parts and whole module – perhaps along the lines of Example 10.2. While it is being studied you can survey

Component	Words/length		Difficulty	Study time
Study guide	Part 1	3000	Easy	30 min
	Part 2	4500	Easy	45 min
	Part 3	4500	Moderate	1 hr 4 min
	Part 4	2000	Difficult	50 min
Set book	Ch. 8	4000	Difficult	1 hr 40 min
Experiment	(15 min/day × 5 days)			45 min
In-text activities	(16 × 2–15 mins, individually assessed)			2 hrs 30 min
Audio cassette	Running time			25 min
	Preparation			10 min
	Exercise			15 min
	Summary task			15 min
Telephone tutorial	Lapse time			45 min
	Preparation			15 min
Assignment				5 hrs 00 min
			Total	14 hrs 49 min

If the teaching material was designed to be equivalent to 12 hours of study time it is over-length!

Example 10.2 *Example of workload estimates*

your learners, determine the success of their learning and the time(s) they spent studying the various components. I think you may be surprised by how accurate you have been in some allocations – and how inaccurate in others!

References

Chambers, E C (1994) Assessing student workload, in *Materials Production in Open and Distance Learning* (ed F. Lockwood), Paul Chapman Publishing, London.

Gunning, R (1968) *The Technique of Clear Writing*, McGraw-Hill, New York.

Henry, J (1994) *Teaching Through Projects*, Kogan Page, London.

International Centre for Distance Learning (1998) *Online database*, Open University, Milton Keynes (http://www-icdl.open.ac.uk).

Klare, G R (1984) Readability, in *Handbooks of Reading Research* (ed P D Pearson), Longman, New York.

Lockwood, F, Williams, I and Roberts, D. (1988) Improving teaching at a distance within the University of the South Pacific, *International Journal of Educational Development*, **8**(3), 265–70.

Lockwood, F G (1989) The evaluation of Open University Preparatory Packages, *Open Learning*, **4**(1), 43–6.

Lowe, R (1993) *Successful Instructional Diagrams*, Kogan Page, London.

Macdonald-Ross, M and Scott, B (1995a) Results of the survey of OU students' reading skills, *Text & Readers Programme, Technical Report No. 3*. IET, Open University, Milton Keynes.

Macdonald-Ross, M and Scott, B. (1995b) The readability of OU foundation courses, *Text & Readers Programme, Technical Report No. 5*. IET, Open University, Milton Keynes.

Mason, R (1994) *Using Communication Media in Open and Flexible Learning*, Kogan Page, London.

Open University (1997a) *Courses Survey 1996. Arts Results*, Institute of Educational Technology Student Research Centre SRC Report No. 108, Open University, Milton Keynes.

Open University (1997b) *Courses Survey 1996. Science Results*, Institute of Educational Technology Student Research Centre SRC Report No. 109, Open University, Milton Keynes.

Open University (1997c) *Courses Survey 1996. Social Science Results*, Institute of Educational Technology Student Research Centre SRC Report No. 110, Open University, Milton Keynes.

Open University (1997d) *Courses Survey 1996. Maths and Computing Results*, Institute of Educational Technology Student Research Centre SRC Report No. 111, Open University, Milton Keynes.

Open University (1997e) *Courses Survey 1996. Technology Faculty Results*, Institute of Educational Technology Student Research Centre SRC Report No. 116, Open University, Milton Keynes.

Open University (1997f) *Courses Survey 1996. School of Education Results*, Institute of Educational Technology Student Research Centre SRC Report No. 114, Open University, Milton Keynes.

Open University (1997g) *Courses Survey 1996. Centre for Modern Languages Results*, Institute of Educational Technology Student Research Centre SRC Report No. 113, Open University, Milton Keynes.

Open University (1997h) *Courses Survey 1996. Open University Business School Results*, Institute of Educational Technology Student Research Centre SRC Report No. 115, Open University, Milton Keynes.

Scott, B and Macdonald-Ross M (1995) A postal survey of OU students' reading skills, *Text & Readers Programme, Technical Report No. 2*. IET, Open University, Milton Keynes.

Woodley, A and Parlett, M (1983) Student drop out, *Teaching at a Distance*, **24**, 2–23.

Index